DATE DUE

DEMCO 38-296

GREAT WRITERS OF THE ENGLISH LANGUAGE

Women Writers

TAFF CREDITS

Executive Editor
Reg Wright

Series Editor
Sue Lyon

Editors
Jude Welton
Sylvia Goulding

Deputy Editors
Alice Peebles
Theresa Donaghey

Features Editors
Geraldine McCaughrean
Emma Foa
Ian Chilvers

Art Editors
Kate Sprawson
Jonathan Alden
Helen James

Designers
Simon Wilder
Frank Landamore

Senior Picture Researchers
Julia Hanson
Vanessa Fletcher
Georgina Barker

Picture Clerk
Vanessa Cawley

Production Controllers
Judy Binning
Tom Helsby

Editorial Secretaries
Fiona Bowser
Sylvia Osborne

Managing Editor
Alan Ross

Editorial Consultant
Maggi McCormick

Publishing Manager
Robert Paulley

Reference Edition Published 1989
Published by Marshall Cavendish Corporation
147 West Merrick Road
Freeport, Long Island
N.Y. 11520

Typeset by Litho Link Ltd., Welshpool
Printed and Bound in Italy by
L.E.G.O. S.p.a. Vicenza

LIBRARY OF CONGRESS
Library of Congress Cataloging-in-Publication Data
Great Writers of the English Language
     p. cm.
    Includes index vol.
    ISBN 1-85435-000-5 (set): $399.95
    1. English literature — History and criticism. 2. English
literature — Stories, plots, etc. 3. American literature — History
and criticism. 4. American literature — Stories, plots, etc.
5. Authors. English — Biography. 6. Authors. American — Biography.
I. Marshall Cavendish Corporation.
PR85.G66 1989
820'.9 – dc19
                                     88-21077
                                       CIP

ISBN 1-85435-000-5 (set)
ISBN 1-85435-008-0 (vol)

GREAT WRITERS OF THE ENGLISH LANGUAGE

Women Writers

Jane Austen

Louisa M. Alcott

Katherine Mansfield

Virginia Woolf

MARSHALL CAVENDISH · NEW YORK · TORONTO · LONDON · SYDNEY

CONTENTS

JANE AUSTEN

◆1775-1817◆

The six most polished, controlled and elegant social comedies to be found in English literature were written by a woman whose personal life remains an enigma. Observing her own leisured social circles, Jane Austen's cool judgement, ironic detachment and refined sentiments give her novels a unique depth and compelling charm. Her 'exquisite touch' and sharp but unintrusive humour earned her the immediate admiration of the greatest writers of her day and her popularity remains undimmed.

A Charming Enigma

The 'real' Jane Austen seems always to elude her readers. Her life appears to have been a picture of tranquillity, untouched by the traumas engulfing Europe, but it gave her ample material for her art.

Jane Austen's novels have been immensely popular since the early decades of the 19th century, yet even now there are many aspects of the author's life that remain completely unknown. We know almost nothing of her emotional life and very little about her thoughts, opinions, tastes, prejudices and personality. What we do know derives largely from three sources: her nephew's memoirs written more than 50 years after her death; her own letters written to her sister Cassandra (who destroyed most of them in her old age); and gossip.

Consequently the portrait that has come to be accepted as the 'real' Jane Austen is essentially a view of her created by her family. Yet that view presents a picture that seems strangely at odds with the author of six of the most polished, ironically witty and perceptive novels in the English language.

Jane Austen was born on 16 December 1775 in the rectory of Steventon in Hampshire, where her father was vicar. The Reverend George Austen was a distinguished classical scholar, spending as much time with his books as his parish duties permitted him. Jane's mother, Cassandra, was a keen gardener, mother of eight children and inordinately proud of her aristocratic relations and heritage – particularly her aristocratic nose. There is little to suggest that she had a close understanding or relationship with her second daughter, Jane.

Jane was the sixth child, two years younger than her sister Cassandra. All the sons – James, Edward, Henry, Francis and Charles – distinguished themselves in later life, though Jane's favourite, Henry was thought to lack application. There was one other brother, 'poor George', the second son, who was fostered out to a family in the neighbouring village of Dean. He is believed to have suffered fits, and was never spoken of and never met any of his brothers or sisters.

The Austens were a happy, lively family, reputedly good-natured and sweet-tempered, and family squabbles were almost unknown. According to the custom

A privileged brother
(right) Jane's brother Edward was adopted by the rich but childless Thomas Knight and his wife. As a wealthy landowner, Edward proved to be 'quite a man of business' and was to support his mother and sisters in later life.

Close confidante
(right) Cassandra remained Jane's lifelong friend and confidante. Mrs Austen said of her daughters, 'If Cassandra were going to have her head cut off, Jane would insist on sharing her fate.'

Key Dates

1775 born 16 December, Steventon

1782 attends Mrs Cawley's school. Nearly dies of fever

1784 attends Mrs Latournelle's Abbey School, Reading

1801 moves to Bath. Probable romance in South Devon

1802 Harris Bigg-Wither proposes

1805 father dies

1806 moves to Clifton, then Southampton

1809 moves to Chawton, Hampshire

1811 *Sense and Sensibility* published

1813 *Pride and Prejudice* published

1814 *Mansfield Park* published

1816 *Emma* published. Health deteriorates

1817 moves to Winchester, 24 May. Dies, 18 July.

of their class and time Jane and Cassandra – 'Jenny' and 'Cassie' to the family – led quite different lives from their brothers. While the boys received a classical education and went riding, hunting and shooting, the girls were schooled in household management and taught the 'feminine arts' of singing, dancing and drawing. Jane in addition learned the piano. At the age of seven she and her sister were packed off to a small school run by a relative, Mrs Cawley – a forbidding, stiff and formal personality. But the school was not a success – possibly because of Mrs Cawley – and in due course moved from Oxford to Southampton. Here, very soon after arriving, both girls fell victim to putrid fever, and had it not been for Jane's hasty despatch home she might well have died.

HAMPSHIRE SOCIAL CIRCLES

Her stay at home, however, was short, for in 1784 she and Cassandra were sent to Mrs Latournelle's Abbey School at Reading. Here Jane spent two pleasant years. Having acquired the rudiments of a young lady's education, she and Cassandra returned to Steventon in 1785. They helped their mother make preserves, syrups, home-made wine and beer, and in the afternoons received instruction from their father. In later life Jane Austen was misleadingly modest about her education, declaring, 'I think I can boast myself with all possible vanity, the most unlearned and uninformed being that ever dared to be an authoress'. In fact she received a thorough grounding in English language

and literature, read fluently in French and had, in addition, a passing acquaintance with Italian.

When the daily duties were done, evenings with the family were spent playing charades round the candle-lit table and then – while the girls and Mrs Austen sewed, darned or embroidered – George, James or Henry Austen would read aloud from their favourite authors; Shakespeare, Dr Johnson, Addison and Steele and the contemporary poet, William Cowper. Sometimes they would read a play with each member of the family taking a part. Occasionally, especially at Christmas, plays would be performed.

As Jane grew into her teens, her closest companion and confidante remained Cassandra. They shared the same interests, enthusiasms and sense of humour. And when household duties permitted, they walked together in the nearby woods or through the pretty Hampshire countryside – the sort of countryside Jane had in mind when she later said, 'The beauties of nature must for me be one of the joys of Heaven'. There were also visits to relatives and family friends. In 1788 she and Cassandra visited their great-uncle in Sevenoaks, Kent where they met their cousin Philadelphia Walters, remembered for her unflattering description of Jane: 'not very pretty and very prim, unlike a girl of twelve'.

Whatever the physical charms of the young Jane Austen, her writings of the time were far from being prim. Before the age of 16 she had filled three notebooks with stories, poems and plays bearing such

Presenting a son
(left) This silhouette shows Jane's father, the Reverend George Austen, presenting his son Edward to Mr and Mrs Thomas Knight. The Knights were a wealthy landowning family; Edward became heir to the family seat at Godmersham Park in Kent and to Chawton Manor, Hampshire.

Steventon Rectory
(below) Jane Austen's home for the first 25 years of her life was in the wooded chalkland of Hampshire.

'The beauties of nature'
(left) Jane Austen loved the quiet beauty of her native Hampshire countryside: "It was a sweet view – sweet to the eye and the mind, English verdure, English culture, English comfort seen under a sun bright without being oppressive."

titles as *The Mystery, Kitty,* or *The Bower, Love and Freindship* – misspelt throughout. Each was dedicated to a different member of the family, and each was a comic burlesque of some contemporary tale.

In common with girls of her class, at the age of 16 Jane was launched into society. This consisted, for the most part, in visiting other families belonging to the same social class – gentry and minor aristocracy; the Jervoices, Terrys, Boltons, Portsmouths, Digwoods and Harrods. Slightly further afield lived the Bigg-Wither family at Manydown House, near Basingstoke, where Jane and Cassandra stayed when attending nearby balls.

Dancing formed a large part of these Hampshire social gatherings, as Jane revealed to Cassandra in a letter of September 1796, 'We dined at Goodestone', she wrote, 'and in the Evening danced two Country Dances and the Boulangeries. I opened the Ball with Edwd Bridges . . .'. Her letters also hint at a number of flirtations which she related to Cassandra in jest. 'At length the day is come', she wrote in one, 'on which I am to flirt my last with Tom Lefroy, and when you receive this it will be over. My tears flow as I write at the melancholy idea'.

There were also visits to Godmersham Park in Kent, where her brother Edward lived. Here, and later at Stoneleigh Abbey in Warwickshire and at Bath, she had a taste of the aristocratic life which was to form the background material for her later novels. While Bath was not the brilliant place it had been earlier in the century, it was still, nevertheless a favourite spot for the fashionable, now denied their visits to Europe because of war with Napoleon. Certainly for Jane there were many distractions and novelties attended by the rich and famous – masquerades, firework displays and fancy dress balls.

COMING OF AGE

Throughout this period Jane Austen continued to write. By 1796 she had completed '*Elinor and Marianne*' (an early version of *Sense and Sensibility*), '*First Impressions*' (the first version of *Pride and Prejudice*) and in 1798 '*Susan*' (later to be called *Northanger Abbey*, set in and around Bath). Unlike the view of her held later, Jane Austen was not at this time a shy and retiring author. Her work was read and appreciated by all the family and was thought sufficiently good by her father for him to offer *First Impressions* to a London publisher. He received no reply. And within the family at least, Jane was not a victim of the false modesty that was said to have afflicted her later in life.

In 1801 the easy, elegant life at Steventon suddenly ended with her father's announcement that on his retirement the family was moving to Bath. Long after her death it was said that Jane fainted on hearing the news. Of the five years spent there we know very little, and only three letters from this period survive, all written to Cassandra. These rare details, together with several critical remarks made later, have led to an assumption that Jane's years at Bath were unhappy. Her unhappiness is thought to have been deepened by an event that might have occurred in the summer of 1801 while holidaying with her parents in South Devon. There she is said to have met and fallen in

The Knights

(left) Mr Thomas Knight and his wife Catherine were continuing a family tradition of patronage to the Austens when they adopted Jane's brother Edward. In 1761, Thomas Knight's father had presented Jane's father with the living of Steventon. Edward was to develop the relationship; he changed his name to Knight in 1812.

Thomas Lefroy

(right) Jane's only 'affair' was with the 'very gentlemanlike, good-looking' Thomas Lefroy. But Lefroy was ambitious and moneyless, and forced to seek a fortune in marriage. The equally moneyless Jane Austen was not suitable.

J. G. Lefroy, Carrigglas Manor, Longford

Chawton Manor

(left) When the widowed Mrs Austen and her daughters decided to leave Southampton, Edward came to their aid. He offered them a house near his own Chawton Manor in Hampshire, which they accepted. They were keen to return to the familiarity of their native locality, and proud to call themselves 'Hampshire-born Austens'.

British Library

Madame de Feuillide

(left) Jane's cousin Eliza shared the Austen's love of theatre, encouraging their family play-acting. Her French husband, the Comte de Feuillide, died on the guillotine after an unsuccessful attempt to save his estates. Despite her knowledge of her cousin's tragedy, Jane Austen's novels never refer to the conflict sweeping Europe.

love with a man whose sudden subsequent death dealt her a blow from which she never fully recovered.

Whatever the truth of this – and there is little to substantiate it – the three letters that do survive do not betray any great unhappiness or dissatisfaction: Jane seems to have continued to join in the general social life of the town. What they do show, however, is a sense of time passing as she approached her thirtieth birthday – as in a letter of 1805: '. . . seven years are enough to change every pore of one's skin and every feeling of one's mind'.

DISRUPTIONS

Certainly there had been changes. She was no longer a young girl. She had been made at least one serious proposal of marriage – by Harris Bigg-Wither, six years her junior, in 1802. After initially accepting the offer, she changed her mind and declined the very next morning. Furthermore, after moving to Bath the family income had been dramatically reduced – with the death of her father in January 1805, financial worries became a constant problem.

Mrs Austen and her two daughters stayed on in Bath another year, though life was now far less agreeable. When they left early in 1806, it was with a feeling of escape, first to Clifton, then to Southampton where they were to live for the next two years. Here, close to brother Frank – now married and pursuing a career in the Royal Navy – life went on as before, with occasional visits to Henry in London and Edward at Godmersham. But Jane's essentially unproductive years continued – no-one quite knows why – until 1809 when she moved to Chawton with her mother and sister, to a cottage provided by Edward close to his Hampshire estate.

Most biographers are agreed that with this move to Chawton, nothing more of significance happened to Jane Austen. By this they mean that there was no major upheaval or event or move to distract her from

THE LOST LOVER?

Suggestions that Jane Austen met and fell in love with a man in either Sidmouth or Teignmouth in 1801 are as veiled and obscure as everything else in her personal life. They are based on a story told by Jane's sister Cassie to her niece Anna – but recollected by Anna's daughter, Mrs Bellas. Neither the age, name or appearance of the young man – if such he was – is known. Nevertheless, the inevitable speculation has ranged from the suggestion that he was a clergyman, to the more colourful suggestion that he was none other than Captain John Wordsworth – the brother of William, the celebrated Lakeland poet – who drowned at sea. It is unlikely that the truth of the matter will ever be known, and we can only guess at the effect it had on the character, and the novels, of Jane Austen.

A rare holiday in Sidmouth, Devon may have led to Jane Austen's only love affair.

Fotomas

Phillips Fine Art

WOMEN, MARRIAGE AND MEN

In Jane Austen's circles, women were almost wholly dependent on men for their survival. Estates were passed from male to male, and only widowed women – who could be bequeathed their husbands' estates – owned property.

Marriage was the only sure way for a woman to gain financial security if, like the Bennets in *Pride and Prejudice*, there were no brothers to inherit the family money. In their case, the estate could *only* be inherited by a male; thus Mrs Bennet is anxious to marry off her daughters.

A man lacking a fortune likewise looked for a suitable marriage, and a prospective wife was more attractive if her husband was to inherit 'her' fortune. The themes in Jane Austen's novels were no different to the realities of her own life – her youthful flirtation with Thomas Lefroy ended when it became known that neither had a fortune. Lefroy's relatives packed him off to Ireland where, after only one year, he became engaged to 'a considerable fortune'. He went on to become Lord Chief Justice of Ireland.

Fortunes changed hands, (right) in Jane Austen's world, when the wedding vows were made.

her chosen path: to remain single and to devote herself to her writing. For whatever the outward events of Jane Austen's life, the real life that she led – the only thing that in the end helped create her art – was that of the imagination. And at Chawton for the seven remaining years of her life, Jane Austen's art suddenly blossomed and reached full maturity.

To all outward appearances she seemed no more than just another refined spinster gentlewoman living with her mother and sister in the country. She dressed in the style of an older woman, generally wearing a cap, symbol of middle-age. All thoughts of an active social life, let alone marriage, seem to have been abandoned. With no carriage at their disposal there was in any case no opportunity to join in the social life of the district. And there was no-one, other than Edward and his family, within walking distance with whom she could have met and spoken as an equal. At Chawton, the Austens kept themselves to themselves.

A QUIET ROUTINE

It was a simple, but fulfilling life, founded on regularity and routine, punctuated by the change of seasons and visits to or from relatives. Mrs Austen spent much of her time in the kitchen garden or at her embroidery, leaving the running of the house to Cassandra. Before breakfast each day, which invariably she prepared, Jane practised at her piano. Until lunch at twelve, she wrote, read or revised her work. After a light lunch, the afternoon was spent in the garden or in walking or shopping at nearby Alton. After an early dinner, the rest of the day was spent playing cards, spillikins, or cup and ball.

The Pump Room, Bath (above) Before moving to Bath in 1801, the Austens had enjoyed several visits to the famous spa resort. Though it was no longer the pinnacle of fashionable high life, Bath still attracted many visitors who now came for health rather than gaiety. Mrs Austen and Jane had accompanied Edward and his family to Bath the previous year, primarily because Edward and his mother were hypochondriacs. According to Jane, 'My mother continues hearty, her appetite & nights are very good, but her Bowels are not entirely settled, & she sometimes complains of an Asthma, a Dropsy, Water in her Chest & a Liver Disorder.' Yet she outlived Jane.

Prince Regent
(right) The Prince admired Jane Austen's works, and kept a set of them in each of his royal houses. Emma was dedicated to him.

Sir Thomas Lawrence 'George IV'/Roy Miles Gallery, Bridgeman Art Library

E. B. Leighton: Signing the Register/City of Bristol Museum and Art Gallery, Bridgeman Art Library

To her nieces and nephews, Jane was an amusing, interesting and animated speaker, subject to fits of laughter. She enjoyed the company of children, and with so many nieces and nephews she was able to enjoy this pleasure to the full.

Hers was a tranquil world, far removed from the traumas engulfing much of Europe. But it was conducive to her art, for in 1811 she published her first book, *Sense and Sensibility*, "by a lady", to be followed by *Pride and Prejudice* (1813), *Mansfield Park* (1814), and in 1816, in the shadow of Waterloo, *Emma*, which received a glowing review from Walter Scott.

But the effort of composition took its toll. She began to suffer from back pains and fits of utter fatigue and weariness. Though undiagnosed at the time, she was suffering from the early stages of Addison's Disease, at that time fatal. The doctors were baffled, and her decline continued. In May 1817 she was advised to move to Winchester to consult a Dr Lyford. Lodgings were found for her in College Street, where she was looked after by the ever-devoted Cassandra. She remained cheerful to the end, joking, writing letters and saying she expected to recover. It was a forlorn hope. Attended by Cassandra night and day, her condition gradually deteriorated. In the third week of July she was told she had not long to live. Calmly she took her leave of each of her relatives in turn. On the evening of 17 July she fell unconscious. At 4.30 in the morning of 18 July 1817, Jane Austen died, her head pillowed on Cassandra's shoulder. She was 41.

Chawton House
(left) Enjoying frequent visits from her beloved nieces and nephews, Jane – with Cassie and Mrs Austen – lived here until 1817.

College Street, Winchester
(below) When it became obvious that Jane was dying, she moved here to receive medical care. She died in Cassandra's arms.

Cephas Picture Library

Mansell Collection

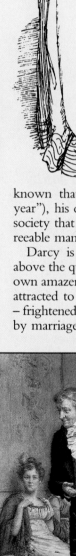

PRIDE AND PREJUDICE

With its proud hero, its vivacious heroine and her excruciatingly embarrassing mother, this delightful social comedy balances humour with an ironic view of civilized Georgian behaviour.

Perhaps the best-loved romantic novel of all time, *Pride and Prejudice* is also one of the most witty social comedies of the 19th century. Jane Austen's unerring sense of irony and genius for dialogue make this light-hearted, elegant love story a subtle examination of the rules and values governing civilized society.

GUIDE TO THE PLOT

The novel revolves around Elizabeth Bennet – an attractive, intelligent, young woman with an independent spirit and a keen sense of humour. She is the second of five daughters of an upper middle-class country family. Although Elizabeth is unconcerned about finding a partner, her mother is desperately eager to marry off her daughters. Her desperation does not lack foundation – the family estate can only be inherited by a male. Unless one of her daughters marries, on the death of Mr Bennet the estate would pass to Mr Collins, a distant relation, leaving the family destitute.

So when a handsome, rich young bachelor, Bingley, arrives at the nearby country estate of Netherfield Park, Mrs Bennet immediately hopes that either Elizabeth or her elder, beautiful sister Jane will win him; "If I can but see one of my daughters happily settled at Netherfield . . . and all the others equally well married, I shall have nothing to wish for." She schemes unashamedly to bring Jane and Bingley together.

> "*It is a truth universally acknowledged, that a single man in possession of a good fortune, must be in want of a wife.*"

At a ball held by another neighbour, the good-natured Bingley dances with Jane twice – an acknowledged indication of interest. At the same ball, Elizabeth meets Bingley's even richer "noble" friend Darcy, but their initial encounter is less promising. She overhears him say that he will not dance with her, because she is "not handsome enough to tempt *me*". And although at first Darcy impresses everyone with his money (it soon becomes known that he is worth "ten thousand a year"), his conceited manners convince local society that he is "the proudest, most disagreeable man in the world".

Darcy is proud. He feels himself to be above the quiet country set. But much to his own amazement, he begins to feel irresistibly attracted to Elizabeth. He fights his feelings – frightened that he will compromise himself by marriage to a girl with little 'breeding'.

The Bennet sisters
(left) Elizabeth and her sister Jane are of an age when their mother is desperate to find husbands for them. But Elizabeth's critical nature and determination only to marry for love leads her to reject two proposals. Jane's good nature mars her chances.

Dancing partners
Dances form the social focus of Austen's romantic world. It is in the ball-room that individuals can become couples: "To be fond of dancing was a certain step to falling in love" Mrs Bennet believes.

Darcy's pride
When Elizabeth and Darcy first meet, he thinks she is "not handsome enough to tempt me". But at a later ball (left), when they are dancing together, the reaction of Elizabeth's neighbour Sir William Lucas reveals the sort of deference which has led to Darcy's proud manner: "Such very superior dancing is not often seen". It takes Elizabeth – and her lack of respect for anyone who does not deserve it – to make Darcy realize the error of his ways.

First Impressions
The original version of Pride and Prejudice *was entitled 'First Impressions' – impressions that are often coloured by prejudice. Elizabeth's first reaction to the charming soldier Wickham is woefully misguided.*

Elizabeth, unaware of Darcy's feelings for her, falls for another new arrival in the district – a charming and "universally liked" young army officer named Wickham. Although she knows nothing about him, she is taken in by his flattering behaviour toward her and believes the awful stories he tells her – he claims that Darcy has deliberately and spitefully ruined his prospects.

While he is telling tales about Darcy, Wickham confides to Elizabeth: "I can never defy or expose him". Wilfully blinding herself to the fact that he is doing exactly that, Elizabeth "honoured him for such feelings, and thought him handsomer than ever as he expressed them".

A day or two later, Elizabeth is completely taken aback to receive a proposal of marriage from her clergyman cousin Mr Collins, the man who is to inherit her father's estate. Elizabeth considers Mr Collins a "conceited, pompous, narrow-minded, silly man", and so rejects him – to his disbelief and despite her mother's protestations. But Elizabeth's friend Charlotte accepts Collins a few days

The elopement
(right) Wickham reveals his true colours when he elopes with the 16 year-old Lydia Bennet. Suddenly, public opinion changes, and everyone "seemed striving to blacken the man, who but three months before, had been almost an angel of light". Darcy also reveals his real character when he saves the Bennet family from disgrace by giving Wickham financial encouragement to marry Lydia.

later – although she does not love him either. Elizabeth is appalled at her friend's sacrifice of love for money, but Charlotte explains "I am not romantic . . . I ask only a comfortable home".

Other shocks follow quickly. Wickham turns his attentions from Elizabeth to a rich heiress, and Bingley leaves the district. Mrs Bennet is distraught, Jane is unhappy and ill, and Elizabeth – still trying to accept Wickham's apparently mercenary behaviour – cannot understand Bingley's departure.

Some months later, Elizabeth learns that Darcy had a part to play in Bingley's separation from Jane – because he thought that Jane's family was not good enough for his friend. Her contempt for Darcy is almost complete, when he suddenly arrives – and proposes. But even in the proposal there is an insult – he declares that he has found it "impossible to conquer" his feelings, despite "his sense of her inferiority". Elizabeth is angered and rejects him, partly because of what she knows (or thinks she knows) about his involvement in separating Bingley and Jane, and his allegedly callous behaviour towards Wickham.

Darcy, with "mingled incredulity and mortification", leaves.

In a letter, he explains the true nature of his involvement with Bingley and Wickham, and for the first time, Elizabeth realizes that she may have been wrong about him – that she may have been as guilty of prejudice as he was of pride. She begins to rethink her attitudes, and comes to realize that Darcy could have "answered all her wishes".

As events unfold, and Wickham is only prevented from bringing disgrace upon the Bennet family by Darcy's secret intervention, Elizabeth learns to lose her prejudice and Darcy his pride. And at last, Mrs Bennet's hopes for her girls look as if they may be fulfilled.

WIT AND HUMOUR
The opening sentence of *Pride and Prejudice* sets the witty, ironic tone of the novel – as well as indicating its major theme: "It is a truth universally acknowledged, that a single man in possession of a good fortune, must be in want of a wife". What this actually means is that "a single man in possession of

British Library

H. B. Sparks: The Squire's Wedding/Fine Art Photographic Library

a good fortune" is a prey to unmarried women. Or as Austen herself writes in the subsequent paragraph:

However little known the feelings or views of such a man may be on his first entering a neighbourhood, the truth is so well fixed in the minds of the surrounding families, that he is considered as the rightful property of some one or other of their daughters.

This is certainly the view of Mrs Bennet, Elizabeth's silly, shallow, neurotic mother whose "business [in] life was to get her

> "'We all know him to be a proud, unpleasant sort of man; but this would be nothing if you really liked him.'
> 'I do, I do like him,' she replied, with tears in her eyes, 'I love him. Indeed he has no improper pride. He is perfectly amiable. You do not know what he really is…'"

The country house
When Elizabeth first sees Darcy's impressive stately home, Pemberley House, she realizes that "to be mistress of Pemberley might be something". It is here that she learns from Darcy's aged servant (and "What praise is more valuable than the praise of an intelligent servant?"), that he has always been good tempered and generous. Elizabeth's opinion of him rapidly changes for the better.

daughters married". Her husband Mr Bennet – who married her for her looks and has long ago lost respect for and fallen out of love with her – treats her with a similar sense of satirical humour to that used by Jane Austen herself. In reply to Mrs Bennet's perennial complaint that "You take delight in vexing me. You have no compassion on my poor nerves", he tells her:

'You mistake me, my dear. I have a high respect for your nerves. They are my old friends. I have heard you mention them with consideration these twenty years at least.'

Austen uses her wit and irony to expose and poke fun at the flaws in her characters' personalities. Mrs Bennet has more than her fair share of flaws, and is considered by her

fellow-characters as well as by her author as a ridiculous, irritating, embarrassing woman. But virtually all the characters in the novel have some deficiency which is treated with anything ranging from gentle, sympathetic humour to cutting satire by Austen.

It is ironic that Elizabeth, who prides herself on her ability to analyze character, should be blinded by prejudice in relation to Darcy and Wickham. She learns a painful lesson that "One has got all the goodness, and the other all the appearance of it". But Austen likes her heroine, and treats her gently. Bingley's cruel, snobbish sisters receive harsher treatment because they had "indulged their mirth for some time at the expense of their dear friend's vulgar relations".

Mr Collins, the pompous, servile and essentially unchristian clergyman is also allowed by Austen to expose his own "mixture of pride and obsequiousness, self-importance and humility". Mr Bennet mercilessly encourages him to do so. When Mr Collins is recounting how he likes to frame compliments for his (obnoxious) patron Lady Catherine de Bourgh, Mr Bennet asks him "whether these pleasing attentions proceed from the impulse of the moment, or are the result of previous study". The irony of the question is completely lost on Collins, who takes the bait and replies:
'They arise chiefly from what is passing at the time, and though I sometimes amuse myself with suggesting and arranging such little elegant

Matchmaking mother
(right) Mrs Bennet is embarrassingly obvious in her attempts to procure husbands for her daughters. Determined to leave Jane and Bingley alone together – to give him a chance to propose – she "sat winking at Elizabeth and Catherine for a considerable time, without making any impression on them". She manages to remove Kitty from the drawing room, and a few minutes later, she pokes her head round the door and calls for Lizzy. But "Mrs Bennet's schemes for this day were ineffectual."

The wedding day
"Happy for all her maternal feelings was the day on which Mrs Bennet got rid of her two most deserving daughters." The response to Darcy and Elizabeth's marriage ranges from pride (Mrs Bennet) to opportunist pleasure (Lydia and Wickham) and extreme indignation (the proud, prejudiced Lady Catherine).

compliments as may be adapted to ordinary occasions, I always wish to give them as unstudied an air as possible.'

Mr Bennet's expectations were fully answered. His cousin was as absurd as he had hoped, and he listened to him with the keenest enjoyment, maintaining at the same time the most resolute composure of countenance . . .

FIRST IMPRESSIONS

The original title of *Pride and Prejudice* was 'First Impressions' – the novel revolves around people's impressions of each other at their first meeting being undermined and altered as their relationships develop.

Elizabeth's first impression of Darcy is that he is handsome. But she soon begins to dislike him, because he speaks badly of the company in general and herself in particular. Then she allows everything she hears and sees to add to her prejudice against him, until – when he has made his insulting proposal – she lets loose all her hatred:

'From the very beginning, from the first moment I may almost say, of my acquaintance with you, your manners impressing me with the fullest belief of your arrogance, your conceit, and your selfish disdain of the feelings of others, were such as to form that ground-work of disapprobation, on which

succeeding events have built so immovable a dislike; and I had not known you a month before I felt that you were the last man in the world whom I could ever be prevailed on to marry.'

But when Darcy's manner towards her changes, Elizabeth changes her mind about him, realizing that their "union" could be "to the advantage of both" – that her "ease and liveliness" might soften his manners, and that she could learn from his judgement.

Darcy is attracted to Elizabeth, but his social standing has made him think that he is too good for her. It takes her rejection of his initial proposal, and her reproof about his ungentleman-like manner in asking for her hand, to make him re-evaluate his view of himself. He was born a 'gentleman', but no-one had ever told him that he did not always act like one. In realizing this about himself, he comes to realize, too, that Elizabeth's worth has less to do with her superficial social standing than with her real nature:

'You taught me a lesson, hard indeed at first, but most advantageous. By you, I was properly humbled. I came to you without a doubt of my reception. You shewed me how insufficient were all of my pretensions to please a woman worthy of being pleased.'

As the hero and heroine slowly and painfully come to revise their first impressions of one another, pride and prejudice give way to love, respect and a successful marriage.

NAPOLEON IGNORED

While Darcy and Elizabeth moved tentatively towards a mutual understanding, Britain was embroiled in a bloody war with France – as Napoleon Bonaparte sought to conquer Europe. Soldiers do appear in *Pride and Prejudice*, but they are figures of seductive gallantry, not fighting men. Austen was well aware of the war – one brother was in the army and two in the navy – but she had no first-hand experience of it, and so wrote nothing of it. For her, the dangers of military manoeuvres lie in making love, not war.

Battle of Waterloo
The Napoleonic Wars came to an end when Napoleon was finally defeated at the Battle of Waterloo in 1815 – two years after Pride and Prejudice *was published.*

R. A. Hillingford: The Battle of Waterloo/Bridgeman Art Library

CHARACTERS IN FOCUS

The characters in *Pride and Prejudice* belong to the upper middle-class or aristocratic society of Georgian England. Most have characteristics which relate to 'pride' and 'prejudice', and through their relationships, Austen examines her central theme of love and marriage. Whether they marry for romantic love, passion, money or mutual respect, each character – and each couple – adds another viewpoint. All are scrutinized with an ironic humour – some are treated gently, some more harshly.

WHO'S WHO

Elizabeth Bennet   The heroine. Vivacious, witty and intelligent, she is also guilty of prejudice in relation to the men in her life.

Jane Bennet   Her beautiful, gentle elder – sister, who is "a great deal too apt . . . to like people in general".

Lydia Bennet   Their pretty, flirtatious and flighty teenage sister.

Kitty and Mary   The youngest Bennet girls.

Mrs Bennet   Their mother. A silly woman, whose only thought is to marry off her daughters.

Mr Bennet   Their father: "a mixture of quick parts, sarcastic humour, reserve and caprice".

Mr Collins   A pompous, sycophantic clergyman due to inherit the Bennet estate.

Charlotte Lucas   Elizabeth's neighbour and close friend, who marries Mr Collins after Elizabeth refuses him.

Bingley   A handsome, eligible bachelor, who is enamoured of Jane, but soon leaves the district.

Mrs Hurst and Miss Bingley   His snobbish sisters, who consider Jane beneath them.

Darcy   The hero. A rich young man, whose "arrogance . . . conceit . . . and disdain" dominate his character – until he meets Elizabeth.

Wickham   A charming soldier, who turns out to be "false, deceitful and insinuating".

Lady Catherine de Bourgh   Darcy's overbearing aunt, and Mr Collins' patroness.

Fine Art Photographic Library

Elizabeth's "lively playful disposition, which delighted in anything ridiculous" makes her one of the most endearing of all romantic heroines. Despite priding herself on her "discernment", she is prejudiced against Darcy and biased towards Wickham – because she has been "pleased by the preference of one, and offended by the neglect of the other". Elizabeth is taken in by Wickham's good looks and attentive behaviour towards her: it was not "in her nature to question the veracity of a young man of such amiable appearance". But as events unfold, she learns that she has been "blind, partial, prejudiced, absurd", while Darcy realizes that he loves her.

City of Bristol Museum and Art Gallery

Mrs Bennet (left) "was a woman of mean understanding, little information, and uncertain temper. When she was discontented, she fancied herself nervous. The business of her life was to get her daughters married; its solace was visiting and news".

Lady Catherine is "the sort of woman whom one cannot regard with too much deference" – or so she and Mr Collins think. A domineering old aristocrat, she believes she knows best for everyone. But her determination to keep Elizabeth and Darcy apart backfires.

Lydia imagines **"tenderly flirting** with at least six officers at once", when she is given permission to stay with an army family in Brighton. Elizabeth warns their father that she will "be the most determined flirt that ever made herself and her family look ridiculous" if he lets her go. Her fears prove well founded.

Fine Art Photographic Library

Christie's/Bridgeman Art Library

A self-important, **clergyman, Mr Collins** (above) is the cousin who stands to inherit the Bennet estate, should the girls not marry. He arrives at the Bennet's home to "secure an amiable companion for myself, with due consideration for the advantage of all your [the Bennet] family", and cannot comprehend Elizabeth's rejection of his proposal: "he persisted in considering her refusals as flattering encouragement". He marries her friend Charlotte.

E. Blair Leighton: On the Threshold/City of Manchester Art Galleries.

Darcy (above) *is* **"haughty,** reserved, and fastidious, and his manners, though well bred, were not inviting". Although he is rich and handsome, Darcy's proud manner turns local society against him. Elizabeth's opinion of him changes, as he reveals his "compassion and honour".

Jane and Bingley are immediately attracted to each other. But the fact that Bingley is "easily guided" (easily manipulated) by his sisters and friend, and that Jane is "blind to the follies and nonsense of others" threatens their happiness.

ELEGANT IRONY

Jane Austen made her own restricted social world the centre of her writing. Her novels have a unique and subtle charm, with an unprecedented mixture of sharpness, fun, wit and wisdom.

Joseph Conrad once asked H. G. Wells, 'What is all this about Jane Austen? What is there *in* her? What is it all about?' Others, similarly bemused, have asked the same questions. For the problem with Jane Austen has been that, while having many devoted admirers, she seems to others to lack sufficient passion. This feeling about her work was perhaps best expressed – in typical robust fashion – by Mark Twain. 'Whenever I take up *Pride and Prejudice* or *Sense and Sensibility*,' he wrote, 'I feel like a barkeeper entering the Kingdom of Heaven.' Those very qualities admired by some devotees – her elegance, poise, wit and ironical cool judgement – are the very features of her work others find off-putting. This attitude, however, is often based on an impression, rather than on first-hand acquaintance. For the 'real' Jane Austen is rather different from the prim novelist of popular legend.

Jane Austen lived in a time of violent change. Her birth, in 1775, coincided with the beginning of the American War of Independence and the perfection of James Watt's steam engine. In her lifetime, England changed from a predominantly rural country to an industrial world power, and Europe was rocked by revolution and war.

Jane Austen's view of the world and of human nature was rooted in the 18th century.

Courtly behaviour
(above left) Jane Austen's men and women are .characteristically well-bred and well-mannered – it is her speciality to expose the folly, pretension and shallowness that are hidden by a mask of politeness.

A country picnic
(left) An innocuous occasion like a country outing becomes – in Austen's hands – a veritable watershed. In Emma, *a picnic is the setting for the arrogant heroine's fall from grace, and marks a turning-point in the novel.*

during a short illness, was ordered to bed and rest from work. 'I decided to read a novel', he later recalled, 'I had long ago read *Sense and Sensibility* and now I thought I would have *Pride and Prejudice* . . . What calm lives they had, those people! No worries about the French Revolution, or the crashing struggle of the Napoleonic Wars. Only manners controlling natural passion so far as they could, together with cultured explanations of any mischances . . .'

It is perfectly true that the 'crashing struggle' of the Napoleonic Wars is not referred to in any of Jane Austen's novels, nor do we find in them any direct reference to the French Revolution. But then she had no first-hand experience of these events. Jane Austen only wrote works of fiction based on closely observed events, people and places known to her intimately. The first rule of good writing, she maintained, was to write about the things you know about.

Using the material she had at first hand, Jane Austen fashioned her art. Nowhere in her novels, for example, does she portray men except in the company of women. And almost all the action of her novels is reported in dialogue – that is, conversation. When anything dramatic upsets the order and calm of the lives of her characters – elopements, illicit sex, duels and death – it occurs off-stage, belonging to a realm beyond her experience.

Jane Austen prized accuracy of detail and what she called credibility. Such qualities give her novels great realism, the feeling that you have seen the places she describes and known her characters personally. When, many years after her death, Alfred Lord Tennyson was

In Britain at least, the century turned its back on the excesses and enthusiasms of the previous century that had led to civil war. Order, and the management of life – both social and individual – according to the dictates of reason rather than emotion was considered necessary to hold in check Man's violent, corrupt and fundamentally volatile nature. With control, balance and decorum – the benefits of civilization – life could be pleasant and enjoyable. Such beliefs had produced a reasonably stable society, benefitting particularly the class into which Jane Austen was born – upper middle-class landed gentry. Comfortable and secure, her ideals and concerns are those of the century into which she was born, and her views are those she inherited from her father, tempered by favourite authors, notably Dr Samuel Johnson.

WRITING FROM EXPERIENCE

Critics have accused Jane Austen of being peculiarly oblivious to the great events occupying the world stage in her lifetime. Such a thought struck Winston Churchill who,

The social milieu
(above) Provincial life was Austen's raw material, and she often uses social gatherings to provide incident, amusement and "adventures". In Northanger Abbey, her heroine, Catherine Morland, is launched, at a ball, "into all the difficulties and all the dangers of a six weeks' residence in Bath."

Flirting couples
(right) Jane Austen is always careful to distinguish between the kind of vivacity that is accompanied by wisdom, and the reckless flirting of a Lydia Bennet.

visiting Lyme Regis in Dorset, he demanded of his guide, '. . . take me to the Cobb and show me the steps from which Louisa Musgrove fell'. To Tennyson, this character in *Persuasion* was so convincingly drawn that he spoke of her as if she was a real person. But Jane Austen's characters triumph by their charm as well as their credibility. Elizabeth Bennet, for one, conquered not only the fictional Darcy, but the real-life Robert Louis Stevenson, who maintained that when she spoke he wanted to go down on his knees.

The novels' major theme is love and marriage. Superficially they are about how young ladies of good background and breeding fall in love and come to make suitable or disastrous marriages. Yet they are not 'romantic' stories – something Charlotte Brontë found wanting in them. 'The passions are perfectly unknown to her', she said of Jane Austen. But in this she was mistaken. For it is not that 'the passions are unknown' to her characters (or to herself), but that they are controlled.

No good ever came from the passionate display of violent emotion. Strong feelings, so destructive of human relations, should always be contained and controlled, never given in to. And those who do give into them – like Marianne who is deserted by Willoughby in *Sense and Sensibility* – are no better for having done so. As Churchill noted, Jane Austen recommends 'manners controlling natural passion'. In a world turned upside down by passions, leading to the bloody battlefields of Europe in her own time, who is to say that she was wrong?

A DEFENCE OF THE NOVEL

Novel writing in Jane Austen's day was considered by some to be, not actually harmful, but essentially trivial and unimportant. Jane Austen was vehement in her defence of her chosen occupation, and was determined that the novel should be taken as seriously as other literary forms. In *Northanger Abbey*, she gives vent to these unconventional views in an impassioned outburst of feeling. The novel, she says, is a work "in which the greatest powers of the mind are displayed . . . the most thorough knowledge of human nature, the happiest delineation of its varieties, the liveliest effusions of wit and humour are conveyed in the best chosen language". Yet, she laments, "there seems almost a general wish decrying the capacity and undervaluing the labour of the novelist". She vividly sums up her commitment to her craft in a letter to her sister Cassandra, who had enquired whether her domestic duties prevented her from attending to the proofs of *Sense and Sensibility*. 'I am never too busy to think of S. & S.', she writes, 'I can no more forget it than a mother can forget her sucking child.'

At Chawton Cottage, seated at the small

J. H. Williams: St. Valentine's Day/Fine Art Photographic Library

folding mahogany writing desk her father had given her, she set out to find the "best chosen language" to express "the most thorough knowledge of human nature", with "wit" and "humour". For though her novels are about love and marriage, they are conceived as comedies. Malice and bitterness sometimes intrude but the wit is withering without being spiteful, and the humour a gentle mocking at human frailty.

But, when vanity, pride, hypocrisy and humbug appear, they are mercilessly exposed and condemned. For in addition to her powers of observation, description and characterization, Jane Austen was a moralist, believing firmly in a moral code by which to judge human conduct. And in this she was following the fundamental tenets of her age and upbringing.

It was a code based on honesty tempered by realism, 'right' judgement and 'good sense'. In each of the novels the heroine only gains her heart's desire after learning – sometimes painfully – self-knowledge. What prevents this knowledge is often delusion, in one

Friends and sisters
(left) In her novels, Jane Austen creates a galaxy of female characters, from the delightful to the odious. The subtlety and intimacy of female relationships is one of the mainsprings of her art. She depicts men solely in relation to women – negotiating the pitfalls of the drawing room rather than the battlefield.

A Gothic novel
Austen's early novel, Northanger Abbey, *displays the impish spirit of her girlhood writings. In it she parodies the popular Gothic novel – in all its melodrama of style and subject – and in particular, Mrs Radcliffe's The Mysteries of Udolpho (below).*

del.ᵗᵃ da una dama.   Birrell incisit.

ISABELLA E MANFREDI.

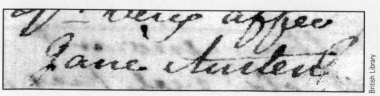

British Library

Letters to a niece
(left) Jane Austen often gave her niece, Anna, advice on novel-writing, stressing the value of accuracy.

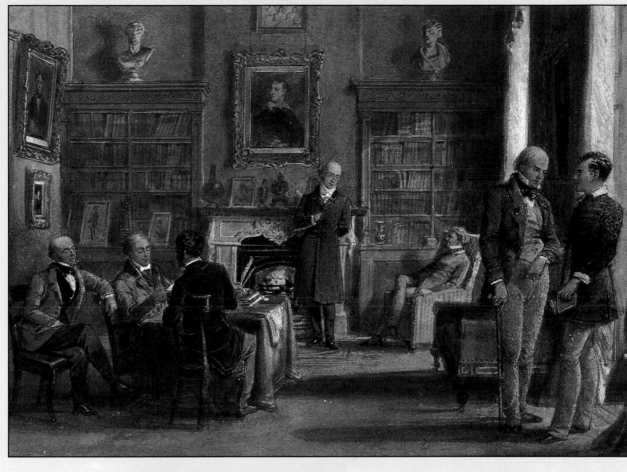

A lady's publisher
(right) Austen offered
Emma to John
Murray, and tried to
fix better terms than she
had previously received.
Although Murray
agreed to share profits,
his new author called
him 'a rogue, of course,
but a civil one'.

First success
(below) Sense and
Sensibility came out in
1811 to some acclaim,
but the author was
anxious to keep her
identity quiet. Yet she
clearly had no wish to
hide her sex, even
though she was
venturing into male
territory.

18th-century style
The poise and precision
of 18th-century writers
such as Dr Samuel
Johnson (below right)
was much admired by
Jane Austen.

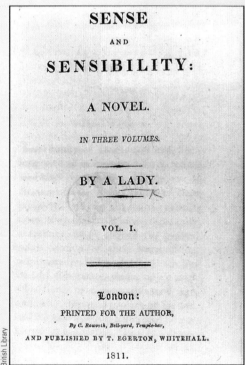

intended meaning goes well beyond the literal meaning. For example, in *Persuasion*, the heroine's father, Sir Walter Elliot, is delicately but firmly put in his place – no "valet of any new made lord [could] be more delighted with the place he held in society". Jane Austen is not content with portraying him as grossly vain and snobbish (which he is), but points out the essential meanness of his aspirations.

Jane Austen's subject matter was strictly circumscribed by the fact that she was a woman. All the opportunities open to her brothers – an Oxford education, foreign travel, financial independence – were denied her. Instead, she lived at home with a demanding and often sick mother, and an understanding, if somewhat intellectually limited sister. Her achievement is the more remarkable given the limited material she had to work with.

After an apprenticeship that had lasted almost 20 years, Jane Austen finally saw her work published, and before her untimely death, achieved recognition. On receiving an advance copy of *Pride and Prejudice* she dashed off a letter to Cassandra, declaring, 'I want to tell you that I have got my own darling child from London . . . I must say that I think her [Elizabeth Bennet] as delightful a creature as ever appeared in print.' Few, least of all Robert Louis Stevenson, would disagree with her.

form or an other. Sometimes, as with Emma Woodhouse, these delusions also concern other people – not seeing them as they really are. This mistake is too often made, Jane Austen says, because of inexperience, inadequate knowledge and superficiality. Only

experience and long association will reveal a person's true nature.

In stating this belief, however, and indeed her own point of view about most things, Jane Austen is rarely obvious or direct. She preferred irony – that is, using words whose

WORKS·IN OUTLINE

For six years from the age of 12, Jane Austen wrote numerous stories all dealing with love and intrigue. Her natural delight in creating fiction incidentally provided her with an ideal training for her mature work. In her juvenilia can already be seen the sharp eye for absurdity and affection which is one of her strengths. Her cheeky humour was to become more ironic and sophisticated, but remained an essential part of her work.

From her girlhood writings, Austen went on to produce three first drafts, which became, in turn, *Sense and Sensibility, Pride and Prejudice* and *Northanger Abbey. Mansfield Park, Emma* and *Persuasion* were original works begun and completed at Chawton between 1811 and 1816. These six major novels were all published between 1813 and 1818.

Virginia Woolf described Austen's novels as 'vivacious, irrepressible, gifted with an invention of great vitality'. Her vitality is all the greater for having nothing more extraordinary to work on than 'three or four families in a country village', their follies, foibles, ambitions and aspirations. Austen modestly likened her art to tiny paintings on ivory, but the exquisite delicacy of her touch has never been equalled.

MANSFIELD PARK

→ 1814 ←

Mansfield Park (above) is the country house in Austen's most serious novel, where young Fanny Price is brought up by her rich uncle Sir Thomas Bertram. Despite Sir Thomas's kindness to her, Fanny is made to feel painfully aware of her humble origins. Of Sir Thomas's children, only Edmund shows

consideration for her, and as Fanny grows up she falls in love with him. In time she becomes indispensable to the Bertram household, and in her gentleness and moral strength highlights the selfishness of her Bertram cousins. The arrival of a glamorous brother and sister from London – Henry and Mary Crawford (left) – triggers a series of intrigues. Edmund is dazzled by Mary, and Henry embarks on a flirtation with Maria Bertram, who is already engaged. Events take a further interesting turn, when Henry transfers his affections to Fanny, and proposes to her. Never attracted by the showy glamour of the Crawford's, Fanny resists – and finally wins Edmund. Austen herself said that the novel had more 'sense' than *Pride and Prejudice*, and certainly its heroine lacks the winning vivacity of Elizabeth Bennet. But *Mansfield Park* shows a real advance in psychological depth and complexity.

SENSE AND SENSIBILITY

→ 1811 ←

Marianne Dashwood (above) epitomizes the quality of sensibility in Jane Austen's first published novel – ."her sorrows, her joys could have no moderation . . . .". She is contrasted with her sister Elinor who possesses "coolness of judgment", and who, though "her feelings were strong . . . knew how to govern them." We see how these differing personalities deal with the problems posed by falling in love. Elinor is attracted to Edward Ferrars, but is cautious in her behaviour; Marianne falls for the feckless John Willoughby, whom she idealizes. Bitter experience teaches her otherwise, but the path of true love proves equally difficult for Elinor; both finally find happiness in unexpected ways.

J. E. Goodall: Preparing for Church/Fine Art Photographic Library

EMMA

✦ 1816 ✦

"**Emma Woodhouse**" (above) "handsome, clever, and rich . . . seemed to unite some of the best blessings of existence . . ." Thus Austen introduces the heroine whom, she said, 'no one but myself will much like'. Over-indulged and bored, Emma undertakes to matchmake for her foolish young protégée, Harriet Smith. At the same time she fancies herself loving, and loved by, Frank Churchill, a newcomer to the area. Emma's mistaken judgement leads to mischief for others and humiliation for herself, all of which is handled with a light but sure comic touch. A perfect example of Austen's wit and irony, *Emma* is unforgettable for its minor characters, notably the awful Mrs Elton and the loquacious spinster Miss Bates.

Mansell Collection

LYME COBB.

NORTHANGER ABBEY

✦ 1818 ✦

The Abbey of the title (inset below), is the ancient seat of the Tilneys, whom the heroine Catherine Morland meets in Bath. Young and likeable, Catherine has an imagination fed on a diet of Gothic romances, especially those of Mrs Radcliffe. Fantasy becomes reality, when Catherine and Henry Tilney fall in love, and she visits Northanger Abbey (below), which she imagines to conceal some dark and convoluted mystery. Henry points out the absurdity of her imaginings, and despite her humiliation, Catherine's innate good sense enables her to grow up gracefully. Begun in 1798, *Northanger Abbey* is Jane Austen's delightful assault on the excesses and melodrama of the Gothic novel and of *The Mysteries of Udolpho* in particular.

J. Atkinson Grimshaw: A Moated House/Fine Art Photographic Library

PERSUASION

✦ 1818 ✦

Lyme Regis (left) forms part of the setting for Austen's last novel, published after her death. Like its predecessors, it is concerned with vanity, pride and true understanding, but the tone is mellower and the irony tempered with tenderness. The action begins some years after Anne Elliot has broken off her engagement to Captain Wentworth on the persuasion of her friend, Lady Russell, and her father, the snobbish Sir William Elliot. The estranged lovers meet again, but remorse, embarrassment and pain complicate their way to a new understanding. The theme of love is treated with a depth and sensitivity unique in Austen's novels, while the heroine is remarkable for being both good and appealing.

In Jane Austen's day, the spas and sea-bathing resorts of England were exciting, fashionable places, where the leisured classes could take care of their health and indulge their pleasures.

For the English gentry at home – that class so brilliantly satirized in her books – Jane Austen's era was a time of unrivalled pleasure and civilized indulgence. London in 1800 was the most opulent, wealthy capital in the world, and English country houses, set amid acres of landscaped parkland and groves of mature trees, were among the most beautiful in Europe. Providing he did not gamble his money away – which happened all too often – the English gentleman faced only two real problems in life: maintaining his health, and staving off boredom. Both these burdens might be lightened at once by a visit to one of the fashionable health resorts to take the waters.

The fashion among the gentry for taking the waters dated back to the reign of Charles II, when the Cavaliers made the spa towns of Epsom, Tunbridge Wells and Bath the liveliest places in the kingdom. But the later years of the 18th century, and the heady days of the Regency, saw the fashion at a peak. With war-torn Europe effectively closed, more people than ever before were discovering the pleasures of elegant resorts such as Cheltenham, Scarborough and, especially, Bath – Jane Austen's home for five years, and the setting of much of *Northanger Abbey* and *Persuasion*. And every year a new resort seemed to spring up.

Each summer, fashionable society would leave be-hind the noise of London or the tranquillity of the country houses, and bowl along the new roads to spend a few invigorating months at the resort then in vogue (or most accessible). Entire families, often accompanied by friends, rented a large house in one of the graceful new terraces and crescents in the resort, leaving their homes empty of all but a few servants for months on end.

'THIS BOASTED SYSTEM'

From a purely medical point of view, taking the waters – whether bathing in them or drinking them – made as much sense as any other health cure then available. It certainly seemed as beneficial as the attentions of a money-minded quack doctor peddling bizarre, and often dangerous, remedies. It also had a pedigree dating back to the Romans and, according to the 18th-century Dr William Falconer of Bath, there were already 1000 treatises prepared to prove its merits beyond doubt.

Jane Austen's hero, Dr Johnson, was sceptical: 'There is nothing in all this boasted system: No, sir; medicated baths can be no better than warm water: their only effect can be that of tepid moisture'. But few shared his doubts; numerous local men of science could show incontrovertibly just how effective the waters of

J. C. Nattes: Sydney Gardens, Bath/Victoria Art Gallery, Bath/Bridgeman Art Library

A stroll on the crescent
(right) Among the greatest pleasures of the fashionable health resort were the regular promenades along the gracious new crescents and streets. As Jane Austen observed in Northanger Abbey, *". . . a fine Sunday in Bath empties every house of its inhabitants, and all the world appears on such an occasion to walk about and tell their acquaintance what a charming day it is." There were friends to meet, acquaintances to renew – and, perhaps, the chance to follow up an encounter at the previous night's ball.*

Fotomas

J. Pollard: Leaving the White Horse, Piccadilly/Fine Art Photographic Library

Leaving London
(above) At the height of the season dozens of coaches would leave London each day to bowl along the new turnpike roads to Bath and other resorts. But the journey was long and arduous; one coach company boasted 'a flying machine to London from Bath, at eleven o'clock every night, which arrives at seven in the evening of next day in London'.

Sydney Gardens, 1805
(left) When she was in Bath, from 1801 to 1806, Jane Austen lived in a handsome new house opposite Sydney Gardens, 'a wide and extensive hexagonal plantation'. These pleasant gardens provided some relief from the bustle of the streets.

'Doctored to death'
(right) When the alternative was the dubious attentions of the quack doctor, taking the waters must have seemed an attractive – and safe – form of medical treatment. But for those not satisfied with water alone, there were always plenty of quacks on hand in the resorts to proffer advice – though in the contemporary Poetical Bath Guide, *a sick man's nurse 'Declared she was shocked that so many should come/To be doctored to death such a distance from home;/At a place where they tell you that water alone/Can cure all distempers that ever were known'.*

Ann Ronan Picture Library

their own town were at curing all manner of illnesses. Taking the waters was at least relatively harmless.

Besides, fashionable society was more than willing to advocate the health value of taking the waters when it was mixed with the delightful round of social activities offered by the leading resorts. Indeed, for most people who went to the spas, taking the waters meant merely sipping a small glass in the Pump Room every now and then. Only the genuinely infirm or the reckless would actually plunge into the pools or drink their contents in any quantity.

For the rest, the attractions of the resorts were primarily social rather than medical. They went for the chance to mingle with the best possible company in pleasant surroundings and indulge in all kinds of fashionable pursuits. Kept away from Europe, there could be few more delightful ways of whiling away the summer months than staying in a resort and getting swept along in the tide of social activities carefully orchestrated by the resort's master of ceremonies.

THE GLITTERING ROUND

Each resort laid on a glittering round of balls, dinners, concerts, and theatrical performances. And there were dinner parties to attend, evening sessions of whist and faro to play, expeditions to local beauty spots to be made and numerous other occasions to keep social diaries permanently full. In between, ladies would fill the day pleasantly, promenading through the elegant streets, dropping into their favourite shops, chatting about the latest novels and exchanging gossip, while the men often went out hunting on their magnificent thoroughbred horses, returning in the evening to tell of their daring leaps and reckless pursuits.

In all the fashionable resorts, every day's activities followed the same regular routine. Early morning would see people taking turns (circulating) around the Pump Room, meeting acquaintances and perhaps sampling the waters. Then there was breakfast, usually in private, but sometimes in the Assembly Rooms or coffee houses where gentlemen would adjourn to read the newspapers. After the morning church service, ladies and gentlemen were free to go shopping, visit the Circulating Library, take a stroll, go for a drive or canter on the downs.

Dinner was taken between two and three-thirty, then everyone dressed up for a gentle promenade until tea-time in the Assembly Rooms. A little time relaxing at home then prepared them for the variety of entertainments on offer.

Glamour, and the possibility of romantic encounters, was an essential part of the appeal of these resorts – which made them a perfect setting for many scenes in Jane Austen's work. *Ruff's History and Guide to Cheltenham* (1803) paints an exotic picture of morning in the Pump Room. 'The sun has no sooner begun to absorb the cool dews of the morning, and the whole sky to be animated with its warmth and influence . . . than the "busy hum" commences at the well. Between six and seven the walks begin to be filled. From seven till nine they are crowded. Here may be seen a galaxy of beauty, which overpowers even Aurora herself. Here, the sparkling eye – the bewitching mien – the elegant costume, which fascinated all beholders at the evening ball – assumes an altered character. The warm glow of the midnight dance is exchanged for the fresh tint of the morning. The brilliant robe, the necklace, the ear drop, and the head-dress, are transformed into an easier, a simpler, and more becoming attire.'

Sometimes introductions to beauties seen in the Pump Room or the Assembly Rooms were made through mutual friends; sometimes they were effected by the master of ceremonies – such as that of Henry Tilney to Catherine Morland in *Northanger Abbey*. But the regular routine, and the constant round of social engagements, meant there were many opportunities for young people to meet and for romances to blossom – routines which were crucial to the eventual reconciliation of Anne Eliot and Captain Wentworth in *Persuasion*. The more staid resorts became places for respectable families to come and find husbands for their daughters, and young men to find wives.

'FIVE AND THIRTY FRIGHTS'

Many men who frequented the resorts regarded themselves as connoisseurs of female beauty, and were apt to express disappointment at the lack of pretty faces on view, like Sir Walter in *Persuasion*. In a brilliantly satirical passage, Sir Walter's own comments damn him and his type: "The worst of Bath was the number of its plain women . . . He had frequently observed, as he walked, that one handsome face would be followed by thirty, or five and thirty frights; and once, as he stood in a shop in Bond-street, he had counted eighty-seven women go by, one after another, without there being a tolerable face among them."

Yet there was an element of truth in Sir Walter's comments, for the most glamorous young women,

Out in the phaeton
(below) Afternoon drives in the best resorts were like fashion parades. Young ladies and gentlemen vied with each other to be seen wearing the very latest London styles.

Benjamin West: The Bathing Place at Ramsgate/Yale Center for British Art, Paul Mellon Collection

Victoria and Albert Museum/Bridgeman Art Library

Cheltenham Art Gallery and Museums/Bridgeman Art Library

The portrait sitting

(above) Like Thomas Gainsborough, who worked in Bath from 1759 to 1774, many portrait painters set up studios in the health resorts to take advantage of wealthy patrons with time on their hands, and during the day a string of friends and relatives would drop in at the studio to watch the artist transform their gouty old uncle into a debonair squire; it was, of course, the artists who created the most flattering pictures – not the most life-like – who received the lucrative commissions.

Bathing at Ramsgate

(above) When the fashion for sea bathing caught on in the late 18th century, men and women bathed naked together. But soon the more respectable resorts introduced bathing wagons where women could bathe 'Safe from the ken Of those impudent men Who wander about on the shore'. Many people still bathed nude, though, which led one writer to complain that Ramsgate attracted visitors who 'seem to have no more sense of decency than South-Sea islanders!'

A view of Cheltenham

(left) Many of the fashionable resorts were set amid beautiful scenery.

and the most fashionable young men would always head for the resort that was in vogue. By Jane Austen's time Bath was no longer 'in'.

In the mid 18th century, Bath had been the queen of the resorts, with a glamour barely matched by London. The social whirl and excitement promoted and directed by Beau Nash had drawn everyone who was anyone to the city. In Smollett's *Humphrey Clinker* (1770), Squire Bramble complains, "Every upstart of fortune, harnessed to the trappings of mode, presents himself at Bath".

But by the time Jane Austen moved there in 1801, the glamour was beginning to fade, and the city was slipping into respectability. Infirm dowagers were now seen more often than bright young things, and it was now bath chairs, not sedan chairs that pulled up outside the Assembly Rooms. It became a place for solid, comfortable country families to frequent and meet other equally solid, well-to-do country families – the kind of society that Jane Austen portrays so sharply in her novels.

For young girls used only to the narrow world of country society, Bath still seemed an exciting place even in Jane Austen's time. In *Northanger Abbey* Jane Austen recalls the thrill of her own first visit to the city in that of the 17-year-old Catherine Morland: "They arrived at Bath. Catherine was all eager delight; – her eyes were here, there, everywhere, as they approached its fine and striking environs, and afterwards drove through those streets which conducted them to the hotel. She was come to be happy, and she felt happy already". The nights at the theatre, balls and concerts in the Assembly Rooms, and all the other activities for which Bath was famed – combined with the frisson of meeting handsome men – seemed to make Bath a delightful place for the innocent.

But the fashionably bored had seen it all before and soon tired of the city. As Isabella comments in *Northanger Abbey*, "'Do you know I get so immoderately sick of Bath . . . though it is vastly well to be here for a few weeks, we would not live here for millions.'" Jane Austen was merciless in her satire of people like these who sneered at innocent pleasure simply because it was *à la mode* to do so. She came to dislike Bath precisely because it was full of people like Isabella.

Just as Bath's fashionableness declined, so the fortunes of other resorts rose and fell. Cheltenham was the favourite around the turn of the century, but Brighton soon outshone it. Brighton became to the opulent days of the Regency what Bath had been to the mid 18th century – glamorous, glittering, fashionable and scandalous.

THE RUSH TO THE SEA

Brighton was part of a new trend in health resorts. It was not a spa but a place to bathe in the sea. Ever since Dr Richard Russell published his book on *The Use of Sea-Water in Diseases of the Glands* in 1754, the idea that sea-bathing was good for you had been gaining more and more adherents, and received a particular boost from royal endorsement. King George III plunged into the sea at Weymouth in 1789, while it was his son George IV, as Prince of Wales and Prince Regent, whose fondness for sea bathing transformed the little village of Brighthelmstone into Brighton – described by Thackeray as 'London plus prawns for breakfast and sea air'.

The idea of sea bathing caught on to such an extent that the seaside resorts soon all but eclipsed the spas.

Sources and Inspiration

The Austens' favourite contemporary poet, William Cowper, captured the mood in his poem *Retirement*, telling how spas were now abandoned and all 'Fly to the coast for daily, nightly joys, And all impatient of dry land, agree. With one consent to rush into the sea.' Jane Austen visited the seaside herself at Lyme and Sidmouth on many occasions, and many scenes in *Persuasion* are set in Lyme.

At first, men and women bathed naked, but as it became more and more popular – and men brought telescopes to spy on the bathing beauties – resorts with any pretensions to respectability began to use bathing machines to ensure modesty. These were wagons with covered steps that allowed bathers to descend into the sea unseen. After the advent of bathing costumes, most resorts had on hand 'dippers' to encourage the more timid to take the plunge, of which the most famous was Brighton's formidable Martha Gunn. Dippers were strong, tough women who took female bathers 'in their parti-coloured dresses, and gently held them to the breakers, which not so gently passed over them'.

In Jane Austen's time, though, most people went to the sea not to bathe but to enjoy the same company and activities they did in the spas or, in the smaller resorts, the fresh sea-air alone. Mr Musgrove is the only character in *Persuasion* to take the plunge at Lyme; Anne and Henrietta are content to stroll to the sea: "They went to the sands, to watch the flowing of the tide, which a fine south-easterly breeze was bringing in with all the grandeur which so flat a shore admitted. They praised the morning; gloried in the sea; sympathized in the delight of the fresh-feeling breeze . . ."

Like the spas, the seaside resorts provided a wealth of opportunities for Jane Austen to observe the kind

of society and people she portrays so accurately. Like the spas, too, they were ripe for the romantic encounters that are so important in her novels – Jane herself may even have fallen in love in Sidmouth in 1801.

But their fashionableness was to survive barely two decades longer than Jane Austen herself, for the coming of the railways in the 1830s enabled millions of people of all classes to visit the seaside. With the beaches overcrowded, and the tone of resorts lowered, fashionable society abandoned them. Sometimes they returned to the English spas, but following Napoleon's defeat and the prospect of safe passage in Europe, they soon began to patronize the even more exclusive spas of Germany. The days of the fashionable English health resort – and the society that frequented them – were all but ended.

Big dippers
(above) At the large sea bathing resorts, big, strong women 'dippers' were on hand to plunge the more timid bathers – both male and female – under the waves.

'The Folly at Brighton'
(below) Although much ridiculed, the Prince Regent's oriental-style Pavilion at Brighton was the centrepiece of the resort that had become the fashionable playground of Europe.

Beau Brummell
(above) From 1800 to 1810, Beau Brummell, described by Hazlitt as 'the greatest of small wits' and by Carlyle as 'a clothes-wearing man', was the arbiter of fashion in resorts such as Brighton, and his style set the tone for the age.

28

LOUISA M. ALCOTT

1832 - 1888

Louisa May Alcott was brought up in a world where a woman's place
was in the home, but she was determined to be 'rich and famous
before I die' and succeeded in her aim through energy and strength
of character as well as talent. Throughout her adult life she had to
support her family, as her father was a utopian dreamer incapable of
earning a normal living. Domestic troubles haunted her to the end,
but the intimate ties of her family life also provided the material for
her greatest book, *Little Women*.

Driven by Duty

Louisa Alcott's life was dominated by her demanding family. Her writings saved them from poverty, and though she found fame she never achieved personal liberty.

Louisa Alcott's extraordinary upbringing, while detrimental to the achievement of personal happiness, gave her the impetus to become, in her own words, 'rich and famous'. It also provided her with the content of her most famous work, *Little Women*, one of the best-selling novels in the history of American literature.

She was born in Boston on 29 November 1832. Her father Amos Bronson Alcott (known as Bronson) was one of America's earliest and most devoted educational reformers. He was a cold, unemotional man, who regarded himself as the standard by which others had to be judged. He exuded morality, and styled his teaching on the belief that children are born morally perfect. In this he differed fundamentally from contemporary educationalists, who regarded children as fallen creatures who had to be beaten into perfection.

A PROBLEM CHILD

Bronson's views were too radical for most parents, so pupils and income were a rarity. His wife Abba not only had to contend with increasing poverty, but also with bringing up the children virtually single-handed, for Bronson spent most of his time studying or making public addresses. One area where they did initially agree was in defining a woman's role. They believed that a woman should concentrate her ambitions on marriage, on providing stability for the family and on setting a good moral example.

Their first daughter, Anna, quickly became Bronson's favourite because she conformed to his ideals. She was obedient and passive, and learned responses such as

'Father, I love you for punishing me', which guaranteed praise. Louisa, on the other hand, was a problem right from the start. Bronson and Abba thought her too emotional and wilful. And Bronson, desirous for his daughters to be 'little women', could find little to praise in her and much to criticize. When Louisa was two, the birth of a younger sister, Elizabeth, meant that she was largely deprived of Abba, until then her only ally.

Louisa was out in the cold, and she resorted to the attention-seeking device of being naughty. Bronson responded by becoming even more dogmatic, which, in turn, induced a profound sense of guilt and worthlessness in Louisa.

The simplistic world of moral opposites – good and bad – in which Louisa was brought up fed directly into her later fiction. She began fighting a daily childhood battle to suppress what her parents convinced her was an impulsive, opinionated personality, and to cultivate an obedient, 'feminine' temperament.

When Louisa was eight, the family (now including a fourth daughter, May) moved to rural New England so that Bronson could be near his philosopher friends, Ralph Waldo Emerson and the brothers John and Henry Thoreau. Louisa loved the move, revelling in

A prosperous city
(below) Boston had a population of about 100,000 when Louisa was born there. It was a cultural as well as commercial centre, with many resident writers.

Mansell Collection

'Marmee'
(above) Louisa's mother, Abigail May (Abba for short) was known to the children as 'Marmee'. She was devoted to her husband, but often found life with him impossible. Louisa inherited her tall build, and thick chestnut hair.

New England childhood
(above) Louisa's difficult home life was made easier to bear when the family moved to the New England countryside she loved.

A philosopher father
Amos Bronson Alcott (1799-1888) was high-minded, but hopelessly impractical in everyday affairs.

Key Dates

1832 born in Boston

1840 family moves to country

1848 family returns to Boston

1855 publishes *Flower Fables*

1858 death of younger sister Elizabeth

1862 becomes a nurse in the Civil War

1864 publishes *Moods*

1865-66 visits Europe

1868 publishes *Little Women*; pays off debts

1871 revisits Europe; publishes *Little Men*

1877 mother dies

1880 adopts niece Lulu on death of sister May

1886 publishes *Jo's Boys*

1888 dies two days after her father

the countryside and her lessons with Henry Thoreau. She, Anna and Elizabeth also helped Abba to run the house. But family tensions continued to run high. Despite considerable debts, the nonconformist Bronson decided that it was immoral to earn money. Abba had to suffer the additional traumas of Bronson renouncing sex and declaring that, in accordance with his visionary aim of self-purification, the family was to survive on apples and bread.

A couple of years later, the Alcotts moved to 'Fruit-lands', a farmhouse in Massachusetts, which Bronson hoped would be his 'paradise on earth'. But this experiment in communal living precipitated a crisis in both the Alcotts' marriage and their finances. Bronson now relinquished family control to Abba; and she, under intolerable pressure, turned to Louisa for support, and imbued her 'strong' daughter with all her own distrust of men and hatred of poverty. Bronson and Abba were henceforward to have intermittent separations, which were often occasioned by his constant search for an 'ideal' way of life.

Bronson's idealism did have positive effects, however. In 1847, he took in a runaway slave and helped him escape to Canada by means of the 'Underground Railway'. He recorded that the episode had shown his children 'the wrongs of the Black man'.

RETURN TO BOSTON

The following year, Abba instigated a move to Boston. After the freedom and beauty of the countryside Louisa felt like a 'caged seagull' in their dingy rooms in town. But she channelled part of her restless energy into staging family theatricals, in which she played the male roles.

At the same time, the burden of family responsibility was inspiring Louisa with the determination to succeed. Hungry for fame and approval, she announced that she was going to be 'rich and famous before I die'. The tomboyish little girl, accustomed to hiding her innermost longings and conflicts, was soon to become the family saviour.

Louisa taught, looked after an elderly invalid, and

started writing short stories and plays. In her stories *Flower Fables,* published when she was 22, Louisa expressed in fairy-tale form, a nightmare dread of being imprisoned in her own sins. But she saw to it that her heroines were always saved at the last by love. Her plays were also informed by sexual anxieties: *The Unloved Wife* and *The Captive of Seville* featured tender heroines confronted by male rogues.

Just as Louisa's interest in Boston's threatreland was developing, poverty forced the Alcotts to move back to New Hampshire. But Louisa stayed only five months before returning to Boston to write and sell stories. She lodged with an aunt, sending money home to her parents; indeed, she poured all her previously directionless energy into paying off the family debts. Ironically, while work increased her independence, her parents' growing financial dependence correspondingly undermined it.

FAMILY TROUBLES

Louisa's budding career as a novelist was temporarily halted by the death of her sister Elizabeth in 1858. Never recovering from an attack of scarlet fever two years previously, she slowly wasted away to a skeleton, watched over by Abba and Louisa. This loss was followed by another, when Louisa's sister Anna decided to marry. Louisa felt betrayed and threatened and wrote in her journal that she would 'never forgive' Anna's husband for taking her sister from her.

But large political events were soon to displace Louisa's depression and private griefs, when the Civil War began in 1861. It appealed both to her temperament and to her liberal beliefs, and as soon as she was called up as a nurse in 1862, her life changed radically. Assigned to the Union Hotel Hospital, Washington, she rose at 6am and spent the day on a ward that was 'cold, damp, dirty, full of vile odors', bathing and feeding soldiers, and dressing their wounds.

Winslow Homer: Sunday Morning in Virginia. Cincinnati Art Museum, John J. Emery Endowment

Library of Congress/BPCC/Aldus Archive

George Eastman House/BPCC/Aldus Archive

Eminent friends
Henry David Thoreau (far left) and Ralph Waldo Emerson (left) were close friends of Louisa's father and much admired by Louisa herself. Emerson (1803-82) was ordained a priest, but left the Church and evolved a mystic philosophy called Transcendentalism, which involved a deep reverence for Nature. He was a much respected figure – in Europe as well as America. Among his followers, the most important was Thoreau (1817-62), who is best known for his book Walden published in 1854. In it he describes how he lived self-sufficiently for two years in the woods at Walden Pond near Concord, New England.

Educational reform

(left) Louisa's father had progressive social views, advocating women's rights as well as novel educational methods. He was forced to close his school after admitting a black child, whose presence caused the parents of his few other pupils to withdraw them. Louisa was also briefly a teacher, but disliked the work.

A childhood memory

(below) Louisa said that 'I became an Abolitionist at a very early age' and declared that one of the reasons was because as a child 'I was saved from drowning . . . by a coloured boy.' This incident is reflected in Little Women, when Amy falls through the ice while she is skating and is rescued by the watchful and steadfast Laurie.

Niels H. Christiansen: Skating at Sunset/Fine Art Photographic Library

Fact or Fiction

THE PILGRIM'S PROGRESS

In *Little Women* the four girls are given copies of John Bunyan's classic, *The Pilgrim's Progress* – "that beautiful old story of the best life ever lived". First published in 1678, it tells of a dream in which the main character – Christian – journeys through many dangers, including a battle with the fiend Apollyon (right), to the Celestial City (Heaven).

Louisa so exhausted herself and lowered her resistance that she contracted typhoid. Doctors then knew only one treatment for it – massive doses of calomel, a mercury compound, which had the most dreadful side-effects. Louisa's gums were soon so sore that she could barely eat. Poisonous mucus dribbled from her mouth; she lost her magnificent, long chestnut hair and some teeth, and for the rest of her life suffered physical seizures in which her joints were ablaze with pain.

Bronson took her home, where she became delirious and began to suffer hallucinations. She believed herself to be alone in a room full of men; an imaginary Spanish husband leapt out at her at night; and she nursed men who died, one after the other.

Better times were on the way, however. While working in the military hospital, she had received a letter from the editor of *Frank Leslie's Illustrated Newspaper* informing her that *Pauline's Passion and Punishment* (a 'blood and thunder' story, as she described it) had won $100 in a competition. Louisa had it published anonymously. For the next five years, she secretly poured her *alter ego* into more of these stories, using the pseudonym A. M. Barnard.

Her health gradually improved and her writing career flourished. In 1863 she earned $600 from her stories alone, and her letters home from the war were published – to praise from, among others, Henry James (father of the novelist). After 15 years of struggle and uncertainty, she found that publishers were fighting for her work. Her dream was coming true that 'I may yet pay all the debts, fix the house, send May to Italy and keep the old folks cosy, as I've said I would so long yet so hopelessly'.

FINANCIAL SUCCESS

In 1864 Louisa wrote *Moods,* one of her few works for an adult readership, which tackled misunderstanding, misplaced love, disappointment and redemption, and criticized the social restraints binding women. With the money she received for this and for her next short story, *The Marble Woman,* Louisa paid off more family debts and bought coal, wood, food and clothing. But she never enjoyed the fame she achieved through her writing, and dodged, as best she could, the increasing number of readers who came to meet her. 'Admire the books but let the woman alone' she pleaded with her 'dear public' in her journal.

In need of a break, Louisa happily accepted an offer, in 1865, to escort a young invalid to Europe – a journey she had dreamed of making since early childhood. Unfortunately it was not all she had hoped, for her charge constantly complained, and the tiring journey reactivated the poisonous mercury deposits in Louisa's body. When she returned home, her limbs seized up and the constant pain made sleep a rare luxury. Nevertheless, she was so determined to manage her parents' household alone that she fired helper after helper. Eventually she collapsed and had to sit out the winter in her darkened room, not re-emerging until 2 May the following year.

This black period was followed by the highpoint in Louisa's writing career. In 1868 she wrote *Little Women,*

rooted Victorian contempt for spinsters. They were dismissed as incomplete, disagreeable failures who had nothing to offer and were best kept out of sight. Louisa alternated between living with her mother (Bronson was often away giving talks round the country) and, when she found her company too oppressive, in nearby rented rooms.

When she was in her forties, Louisa, now a reticent celebrity, gave her support to the emerging suffragette movement, a natural outlet for her well-informed sympathy for the plight of women. She also helped some friends set up a hospital specializing in alternative medicine, and travelled to feminist meetings in Syracuse and New York, paying her way by writing. But duty kept her increasingly at home, where she nursed her sick and elderly mother.

A DEVASTATING LOSS

Louisa sat with Abba, reading aloud from her own books, the family 'chambermaid and moneymaker', as she described herself. 'I keep at it, and can be a prop, if not an angel, in the house.' But she was still torn by the conflicts of duty and private needs, and wrote, 'I ought to be contented with knowing I help . . . But I'm selfish, and want to go away and rest in Europe. Never shall.' (Louisa had revisited Europe in 1871 but, as she predicted, was never to go there again.)

The physical and emotional strain of caring for Abba made Louisa so ill that Anna had to look after both of them. When Abba died in 1877, Louisa was relieved that she had not suffered, but wrote: 'I shall be glad to follow her. I never wish her back, but a great warmth

a private attempt to rework and understand her childhood. She wrestled with her early conflicts, locked away in her room for hours at a time, while her parents read and talked downstairs.

Little Women was an instant hit, providing royalties of $8,500 within the year, and leading a triumphant Louisa to write in her journal: 'Paid up all the debts . . . thank the Lord! . . . Now I think I could die in peace.' However, although the book was such a success it also represented a disastrous artistic 'road block'. It confirmed Louisa's role as the Alcott's financial saviour, but thwarted her attempts to develop as a writer. Her readers so loved the world of *Little Women* that they demanded more and more of the same. That was what Louisa gave them, churning out a stream of such 'heart-warming' stories. When, in 1870, Anna's husband died, Louisa responded by writing *Little Men* and giving the profits to her sister.

Louisa's selfless commitment to live for and through her family made her increasingly the victim of the deep-

Europe at last

(above) In 1865-66 Louisa made a journey to Europe as a companion to an invalid. Much of the time was spent in Nice, in the sunshine of the Riviera. The place was a delight, but the invalid was trying.

A nurse at war

(right) Louisa worked nobly as a nurse during the American Civil War, but paid a heavy price for her devotion, contracting an illness that was to affect her health for the rest of her life.'

THE SHY SUFFRAGETTE

L ouisa took a personal, practical interest in the two major political events of her time: she was a nurse in the Civil War and later joined the women's suffrage movement, knowing the plight of women expected to fulfil predetermined roles.

She attended many of the early feminists' meetings, but always as a private individual, never as the celebrated writer. In October 1875, however, she paid the price of her fame while attending the Women's Congress at Syracuse in New York State. Much too shy to speak, Louisa sat at the back until, on the last day, she arrived too late to find a seat and had to sit on stage. She was immediately recognized, and when the speeches were over was surrounded by autograph hunters. Louisa hated this kind of attention and fled the hall as soon as she could.

Votes for women!
The women's suffrage movement was active on both sides of the Atlantic. Although its militant protests have become famous, humour was also an effective weapon.

Mansell Collection

Family ties
When Louisa's sister May (below left) died in 1880 after giving birth to a daughter, Louisa adopted the child (below). The little girl was called Louisa May, or Lulu for short. Louisa's devotion to her niece was complete, and she wrote: 'My heart is full of pride and joy, and the touch of her dear little hands seems to take away the bitterness of grief.' But looking after her elderly father as well as the child was too much for Louisa, and in 1884 her sister Anna took over responsibility for Lulu.

seems gone out of life, and there is no motive to go on now.' Two days after the funeral, Louisa and Bronson sat in silence through their respective 45th and 78th birthdays.

Louisa was devastated by the loss of the intense intimacy she had shared with her mother. In her final years, she made her father her primary responsibility, and drew comfort from a new closeness to him. But without Abba, life for both of them had become empty. In 1878 her youngest sister May married and went to live in Paris. Louisa described her as being 'so happy and blest. She always had the cream of things . . . My time is yet to come somewhere else, when I am ready for it.'

Two years later, May died shortly after childbirth, and Louisa took in her baby daughter, Lulu. Although Louisa dearly loved her niece and spent four years caring for her, she finally could not meet the demands made by the little girl. When Bronson was paralyzed by a stroke, Louisa had to give up the struggle and leave Lulu in her sister Anna's care.

DEVOTED TO THE END

Bronson was stronger than the doctors realized, and lived on, a demanding, child-like invalid, for six years. Louisa nursed him with characteristic zeal, while continuing to work. But she herself was physically weak, and the attempt to write *Jo's Boys* brought on an attack of vertigo that kept her in bed for a week. Louisa wrote on against medical advice, and finished the story in 1886. It was the last novel she ever wrote, but it was just

Courtesy of the Louisa May Alcott Memorial Association

as popular as its predecessors, with a first print-run of 50,000 copies.

On Bronson's 86th birthday, Louisa wrote him a touching poem in which she addressed him as a "dear pilgrim" and showed how much she had come to understand him. He died six months later, and Louisa, with her last reason for living now gone, gave up her own long fight against illness. She died just two days after her father, on 6 March 1888. Father and daughter were given a joint funeral, and a moving tribute was paid to them both – he for his philosophic vision, and she for her indisputable literary achievement. She is buried on Author's Hill in the Sleepy Hollow Cemetery in Concord, near Boston, close to the graves of Emerson and Thoreau.

LITTLE WOMEN

The story of four girls growing up during the American Civil War captivated readers when it was first published. And the reassuringly simple world it evokes has made it a timeless classic.

A disarmingly simple and heart-warming tale, *Little Women* tells the story of four girls and their mother during one year of the American Civil War. Adolescent crises and dramas are described with tenderness and humour as the author explores the trials and joys of growing up in a home short of money but rich in love. The personalities of the four sisters incorporate universal virtues and weaknesses with which it is easy to identify. As the girls make their journey towards adulthood, the story is filled with moments of intense pathos, contrasted with wonderfully joyful events that serve to remind us "there is

but their mother encourages, in particular, a game based on *The Pilgrim's Progress*.

She gives them each a copy of Bunyan's allegorical tale for Christmas, and the sisters seek to become real-life pilgrims, using the example of Bunyan's 'Christian' to help them overcome their individual trials and burdens. Rather than being a continuous narrative, the March girls' story is told in a series of almost self-contained episodes, like a television family drama, each episode with its own moral point, and lavishly imbued with tear-jerking sentiment and emotion.

Although poor themselves, the girls offer

A moral lesson
(right) In the chapter entitled 'Jo meets Apollyon', Jo learns the importance of controlling her temper. Amy has spitefully burnt the book Jo has been writing. Jo has "cherished her anger" against her sister, and ignores Amy when she follows her on to the ice (because she intends to apologize). Amy falls through the ice, Laurie rescues her, and a remorseful Jo learns a painful lesson in forgiveness. The 'Apollyon' of the title is a 'foul fiend' of Hell – symbol of Jo's vice, a quick temper.

Mary Evans Picture Library

Mother and daughters
(right) With her husband away at the War, Mrs March – 'Marmee' – looks after her four daughters with the help of their servant Hannah. Marmee personifies the image of perfect motherhood. The four girls – Meg, Jo, Beth and Amy – adore her, and try hard to live up to her virtuous example. They do not always succeed. At the beginning of the story, they gather around Marmee to listen to a letter from Papa who encourages them to be loving, dutiful "little women".

M. E. Gray. Little Women. Hodder & Stoughton/McMullen Collection

always light behind the clouds".

The moral framework of the story is a straightforward one – based on the 'Christian virtues' of goodness and self-denial.

GUIDE TO THE PLOT

Meg, Jo, Beth and Amy March live with their mother and servant Hannah, on modest means after a reverse in their father's fortunes many years before. Papa has gone as a chaplain to the Yankee front, leaving their mother, 'Marmee', to hold the family together in his absence. The girls are highly creative and inventive in making their own entertainment,

their simple Christmas breakfast to the destitute Hummel family living nearby. They are rewarded that same day with ice-cream and cake for supper, courtesy of old Mr Laurence from the grand house next-door. Harumscarum Jo begins her life-long friendship with Laurie, his grandson, by boldly inviting herself round to cheer him up after a week's illness. She disarms the crusty Mr Laurence with her "odd blunt ways", and Laurie is allowed to move freely in the company of the March girls from then on.

The March family's gradual involvement with their wealthy and generous neighbours

greatly enriches their lives. Timid little Beth, "the musical one", reawakens Mr Laurence's most tender memories of the granddaughter he lost many years before. He encourages Beth to make use of the grand piano in his great drawing room, and secretly leaves his study door open so that he can hear her play. When she makes him a pair of embroidered slippers, he responds by giving her a gift beyond her wildest dreams.

Pretty 16-year-old Meg, the eldest, yearns for fine clothes and an idle life, but she contributes to the family income by working as a governess – a job she loathes. She gets a taste

of a more glamorous way of life when she is invited for a week to stay with the wealthy Moffat family. Although it seems that Meg's head is turned by luxury and indulgence at "Vanity Fair", the Moffats' small-minded and vulgar preoccupations with ball-gowns and match-making eventually make her long for the simple comforts of home. When romance does finally come to Meg, it is from an unexpected, unglamorous source.

'Tomboy' Jo finds a friend her own age to 'lark' with, and she and Laurie become inseparable. Jo's heaviest burden as a pilgrim is to act as companion to bad-tempered Aunt March, but she learns to shoulder the task with characteristic good humour. She also learns to control her quick temper when a skating accident involving her youngest sister Amy brings home to her the importance of never letting the sun go down on her anger. Jo's fierce desire to become a writer leads her to spend hours in the garret with her pet rat, writing poems and plays for the amusement

M. E. Gray: Jo and Mr. Laurence. Hodder & Stoughton/McMullen Collection

of the family, eventually managing to make a first mark on the world of letters.

Dark days descend on the March household when a telegram summons their mother to the bedside of her husband who lies gravely ill. With faithful Hannah's care, the girls keep house as best they can under the kind protection of the Laurences. Then Beth falls ill with scarlet fever, which she picked up when she was selflessly visiting the Hummel family's dying baby.

Everyone is devastated at the possibility of losing Beth, none more than Jo, who cries, "Beth is my conscience, and I *can't* give her up. I can't! I can't." Their secure world seems to be threatened on all sides. Will the little pilgrims escape from the shadows of "Dark Days" into the sunshine of "Pleasant Meadows"?

A FAMILY DRAMA

Louisa May Alcott described her book as 'a domestic drama'. She creates a vivid picture of mid-19th-century home life among the impoverished, genteel middle-class family – their clothing, social etiquette, food, letter-writing and Christmas rituals. It is a closed, circumscribed, female world where the darning of stockings, flower arrangement and hot turnovers for breakfast form the backdrop to the 'drama'.

On publication, the story was adopted almost immediately as a children's classic, enjoyed for its whole-hearted celebration of family life and praise of godly virtues. It was considered especially suitable for girls. More than a century later, the book continues to be a best-seller, inviting readers to believe in a

Poor neighbours
The girls try to help the poor Hummel family, but are no match for the horrors of destitution.

Thomas Brooks: Charity (detail)/Fine Art Photographic Library

"*I know they will remember all I said to them, that they will be loving children to you, will do their duty faithfully, fight their bosom enemies bravely, and conquer themselves so beautifully, that when I come back to them I may be fonder and prouder than ever of my little women.*"

Rich neighbours
(above) When Jo is visiting the rich-but-lonely boy next door, Laurie, she meets his awesome grandfather, Mr Laurence. Initially "a little bit afraid of him", she learns that his gruff exterior hides a kind and generous heart. He gives both financial and emotional support to the Marches.

well-ordered universe where self-sacrifice and the struggle to be good are always rewarded. When Alcott set out to write a book which would appeal to a young readership, she wrote an account of the adolescence and family life she herself *wished* she had experienced.

Jo, who quickly becomes the central character, is based very much on Alcott's own vision of herself at that age. Jo abounds with rebellion, creative energy and fiery ambition, fuelled by a frustration at being born female:
'I hate to think I've got to grow up, and be Miss March, and wear long gowns, and look as prim as a China-aster! I can't get over my disappointment in not being a boy.'

SELF-DENIAL AND REWARD
Of all the themes present in the book, self-denial and self-control among "little women" are the most pervasive. These are synonymous with a woman's role in life, and essential to 19th-century ideas of femininity. Marmee, the 'perfect' mother, always gentle, soft-spoken and kind, reveals to Jo her lifelong struggle to control her temper:
'I am angry nearly every day of my life, Jo; but I have learned not to show it; and I still hope to learn not to feel it, though it may take me another forty years to do so.'

Meg must learn that true, lasting domestic happiness does not depend on vast inherited wealth but in being "happy, beloved and contented" with whatever fate affords. Her reward is "being chosen by a good man", for whom she will have to wait a further three years while he makes a secure living. The sharp boundary between the sexes is made all the more plain by her lover's comment: " 'You have only to wait; *I* have to do the work.' "

Beth, the gentle darling of the family, rarely leaves the house, preferring to "keep home neat and comfortable for the workers, never thinking of any reward but to be loved". Her only real longing is to improve her music – a wish no sooner expressed than granted. Beth is almost too good for this world, her self-denial extreme enough to render her near-invisible to the others on occasions. Her brush with death frightens everyone into awareness, however, and Beth's subsequent invalid status ensures that she will be cared for and pampered like one of her own dolls or kittens.

Silly, vain little Amy, whose flat nose is the

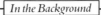

> *"Jo's ambition was to do something very splendid; what it was she had no idea, as yet, but left it for time to tell her."*

greatest trial of her life, suffers countless daily humiliations by having to wear cast-off clothes and by lacking the pocket money she needs to buy her quota of pickled limes for the girls at school. Marmee faces a hard task in persuading Amy of the virtues of humility and sacrifice, but slowly the 'little Madam' achieves a childish desire to be less selfish, and earns her mother's praise: " '. . .do your best; I think you will prosper, for the sincere wish to be good is half the battle.' " But Alcott clearly felt a certain ambivalence about Amy's nature.

It is Jo who undergoes the major struggles in trying to match up to her parents' expectations. When she cuts and sells her hair (her "one beauty") in order to finance her mother's trip to her father, everyone is alarmed at the

M. E. Gray: The Crisis. Hodder & Stoughton/McMullen Collection

---

| *In the Background* |

SCARLET FEVER
Scarlet fever, so called because of the bright red rash that appears on the skin of the patient, is an acute infectious disease, most common in young children. Known in Europe since the early 17th century, it had travelled to North America by about 1735. The disease could be spread in various ways – by dust particles, for example, as well as by direct contact with the sufferer, and through contaminated food and drink.

Before the discovery of penicillin, scarlet fever often proved fatal. Louisa's own sister – Elizabeth – died from it.

Dark Days
Beth's sufferings are pathetic: "It was a piteous sight – the once busy hands so weak and wasted, the once smiling lips quite dumb . . ."

Ellen Jolin: Picking Flowers. Christie's, London/Bridgeman Art Library

"Being chosen"

(right) Meg receives a tender offer of marriage from a "truly excellent young man". But Jo is upset that her elder sister might be leaving the fold: "'I just wish I could marry Meg myself, and keep her safe in the family'", she says.

Picnic in the meadow

(left) One morning, Jo receives a note from Laurie: "Dear Jo, What ho! . . . Some English boys and girls are coming". The sisters join Laurie and his wealthy friends for a day of picnicking, croquet, storytelling and a revealing game called 'Truth'.

Getting published

(below) Like Louisa May herself, Jo aims to make an independent career as a writer. When her first story, 'The Rival Painters', is published, Jo declares: "I am so happy, for in time I may be able to support myself and the girls'".

extreme nature of the act. With her hair goes something of her strength and spirit; her face "has grown gentler and her voice is lower; she doesn't bounce, but moves quietly . . ."

As *Little Women* draws to a close, Meg approaches a happy marriage, Beth has become enshrined in virtuous passivity, Amy has shed some of her selfishness, and Jo, the wild girl, is tamed. All are learning the sweetness of self-denial that is supposed to attend womanhood. For Alcott intended *Little Women* to be a moral tale, echoing Bunyan's original allegory. Their idealized journey towards goodness and adulthood is destined to continue in the popular sequels that followed the enthusiastic reception of "the first act of the domestic drama called LITTLE WOMEN."

CHARACTERS IN FOCUS

The four 'little women' personify particular moral strengths and weaknesses, including impulsive generosity, quiet courage, foolish longings, vanity and selfishness, and yet they never cease to be flesh-and-blood children. From Jo. with her tomboyish enthusiasm, to Beth, with her shy and gentle sweetness, they form some of the most memorable characters of children's literature.

WHO'S WHO

Mrs March Adored 'Marmee', the girls' mother, confidante and friend.

Mr March Symbol of all that is good, the absent father. For him, the girls strive to be brave and dutiful.

Meg Gentle and sensitive, the eldest daughter, who suffers in remembering better times.

Jo The wild one of the family – impetuous, quick-tempered and passionately loyal.

Beth The shy darling of the family, whose near death from scarlet fever shocks everyone.

Amy Full of airs and graces and mispronounced long words, the youngest, wilful 'little Madam'.

Aunt March The elderly rich relative who hides her fondness for the girls behind "rules and orders . . . and long prosy talks".

Laurie Jo's friend, the dark-eyed boy next door, prone to idleness but full of fun and mischief.

Mr Laurence Tall and proud, the neighbour whose reserve is slowly melted by the warmth of the March family.

Hannah Strict, plain speaking and loyal, "Hannah is a model servant and guards pretty Meg like a dragon".

The Moffats "Not particularly cultivated or intelligent people" whose superficial world of parties and fine clothes contrasts sharply with the homely, loving values of the March household.

John Brooke Laurie's soft brown-eyed tutor who falls in love with and proposes to Meg.

H. Knight: The Hammock/Fine Art Photographic Library

"A tall, motherly lady" . . . *"the most splendid mother in the world", Marmee* (right) is a "noble-looking woman", the strength of her inner qualities shining through and showing in her face and bearing. To her daughters she is the essence of perfect motherhood, who cares for them, protects them and guides them through good times and bad. She is the spiritual and moral arbiter of the book and the underlying strength of the family.

G. E. Hicks: War of the Roses/Fine Art Photographic Library

William Holman Hunt: Portrait/Fine Art Photographic Library

Meg is the eldest of the 'little women' (above), Marmee's "pretty, tender-hearted girl" who combines youthful demureness and femininity with a longing for a more dashing lifestyle. "I know I'm a silly little girl . . . But it *is* nice to be praised and admired."

"Jo found her greatest affliction in the fact that she couldn't read, run, and ride as much as she liked" (left). And yet a letter from her beloved father prompts her to exclaim: "'I'll try and be what he loves to call me, "a little woman", and not be rough and wild; but do my duty here instead of wanting to be somewhere else', . . . thinking that keeping her temper at home was a much harder task than facing a rebel or two down South."

On seeing a portrait of Mr. Laurence (right), Jo comments, "'I'm sure now that I shouldn't be afraid of him, for he's got kind eyes,'" and the reality turns out to be even kinder. Mr Laurence is the rich, elderly neighbour who is winkled out of his reclusiveness by the friendly overtures of Jo, Beth and Mrs March. And he turns out to be not merely a friend to them, but also a generous benefactor.

B. W. Leader: Self Portrait/Fine Art Photographic Library

Beth (right) is known as "Little Tranquillity" . . . "for she seemed to live in a happy world of her own, only venturing out to meet the few whom she trusted and loved". She has the status of near-saint in the family. Amy (near right), as the baby of the household, "was in a fair way to be spoilt, for everyone petted her".

Fine Art Photographs

McMullen Collection

Friend, neighbour and fellow-conspirator of Jo, Laurie (above) is both boisterous and lazy. Never one for great industry, he "lay luxuriously swinging to and fro in his hammock". "The hot weather made him indolent, and he had shirked his studies, tried Mr Brooke's patience . . . displeased his grandfather . . . and frightened the maidservants half out of their wits by mischievously hinting that one of his dogs was going mad."

A MASK OF SENTIMENT

Louisa May Alcott had a secret career. Under the pseudonym A.M. Barnard, she rejected her wholesome family sagas in favour of lurid tales of power, passion and revenge.

As a teenager, Louisa May Alcott vowed that she would do something with her life: 'Don't care what – teach, sew, act, write, anything to help the family.' But her compulsion 'to help the family' was probably less of a motive for writing than a justification for it. For her overwhelming need to write might otherwise have made her feel deeply guilty.

Even after *Little Women* 'came home, heavily laden with an unexpected cargo of gold and glory', she found new dutiful reasons for writing. When her brother-in-law John Pratt died, he left his wife Anna and their children ·well provided for, as Louisa very well knew. She nevertheless began *Little Men,* so that, as she claimed, 'John's death may not leave Anna and the dear boys in want'.

At the end of a writing life during which she earned about $200,000, Louisa Alcott was still the family workhorse, arguing that 'Work is and always has been my salvation and I thank the Lord for inventing it.'

Louisa's creative, rather than just financial, impulse to write was obvious from the stories, poems and melodramas she produced as a girl. Her teenage fairy stories were published as *Flower Fables*, when she had just

turned 22. But the family's economic straits certainly influenced her early career. Like a good professional, she studied the possible markets for her work, gaining a foothold on the *Saturday Evening Gazette* in 1854 with $10 worth of what she described as 'rubbish' – 'The Rival Prima Donnas'. This lurid story of two rival singers, one of whom kills the other by crushing her head in a iron ring, was the first of many she wrote for the *Gazette*.

It was not until 1860 that Louisa was published in the prestigious *Atlantic Monthly,* with a moralistic story about a young girl's attempted suicide entitled 'Love and Self-love'. The event prompted an uncharacteristically confident outburst: 'People seem to think it a great thing to get into the *Atlantic:* but I've not been pegging away all these years in vain, and may yet have books and publishers and a fortune of my own.'

THE DARK SIDE

Louisa was developing two careers – one serious and respectable, the other as the writer of 'blood-and-thunder' sensational thrillers. Her work was to divide even more dramatically. In 1862, she entered a competition run by the sensationalist New York magazine *Frank Les-*

A passion for fashion

(right) Louisa had a love of finery that she rarely admitted and never indulged, but expressed instead through her books. She would have loved to have worn clothes such as the femmes fatales *of her thrillers elegantly sported. But the Alcotts could never afford such 'frivolities' and years of self-denial took their toll on Louisa, so that when she became famous and Paris fashions were within her reach, she continued to dress modestly.*

Alias A.M. Barnard

(below and below right) In Pauline's Passion and Punishment, *the heroine is a jealous, angry woman, bent on destroying the lover who has spurned her. The gulf between Pauline and the idealized women in the novels published under Louisa's own name was so wide that she never publicly admitted to the common authorship.*

Weidenfeld Archive

Henry Nelson O'Neill: Sleep/Fine Art Photographic Library

Motherly love

(left) In Louisa's stories for children, she dwells on the virtues of family life – of simplicity, self-sacrifice and tenderness. The bonds between mother and daughter and the loyalty among the children represent bulwarks against all the trials that may beset a family; and if those ties are strong enough, nothing, no matter how terrible, can ultimately hurt them.

Harvard College Library

PRIZE STORY.
PAULINE'S PASSION
AND
PUNISHMENT.
CHAPTER I.

O and iro, like a wild creature in its cage, paced that handsome woman, with bent head, locked hands and restless steps. Some mental storm, swift and sudden as a tempest of the tropics,

War writings

(above) As a nurse in the Civil War, Louisa had to feed, wash and care for dozens of young men in an intimacy far greater than anything she had ever experienced. The horror she went through haunted her. However, her observations, published as Hospital Sketches *(1863), were a huge success. At her request, her publishers set aside 5 cents from every copy sold to care for war orphans.*

there . . . And what would my own good father think of me . . . if I set folks to doing the things that I have a longing to see my people do?'

When the success of *Little Women* in 1868 made Louisa the idol of American girlhood, A.M. Barnard's career came to an end. Indeed, their names were never linked until many years after her death.

Little Women also cut short Louisa's career as a serious novelist for adults rather than children. In August 1860 she had drafted her first novel, *Moods,* 'in a vortex' – a four-week, day-and-night delirium of writing. Later it was extensively revised, and Louisa was inclined to blame its faults on the many advisers she had mistakenly tried to please. It is possible, however, that this was simply a way of disclaiming *Moods,* which gives a less rosy version of her family life than the later works. The curious resolution of the book's eternal triangle (the heroine abandons both husband *and* lover) caused some controversy when it was published in 1864, but now its interest is mainly biographical. The same is true of her later novel *Work,* in which she deals with suicide and frustrated love.

HAMPERED BY SUCCESS

How far Louisa might have developed as a writer for adults will never be known. As late as 1887 she declared that 'I yet hope to write a few of the novels which have been simmering in my brain while necessity & unexpected success have confined me to juvenile literature.'

The 'necessity' was largely self-created, although it is true that both publishers and the general public clamoured for more and more stories in the *Little Women* vein. Despite any reservations she may have had, 'juvenile literature' provided Louisa Alcott with the ideal

lie's Illustrated Newspaper. She won the $100 prize for her story 'Pauline's Passion and Punishment', a tale of love, mystery and violent revenge. It was published anonymously, and started Louisa on a secret career. Adopting the pseudonym 'A.M. Barnard', she became the writer of gruesome, melodramatic magazine thrillers and novelettes.

The A.M. Barnard stories helped the Alcott family budget by bringing in $50 or $75 a time. They also provided an emotional outlet for Louisa herself. Her glamorous heroines allowed her to indulge her interest in wickedly luxurious clothes, which her strict puritan code forbad her to wear. And the angry, vengeful, sexually devastating *femmes*

fatales such as Pauline and 'V.V.' (who wears her initials tattooed on her arm above a lover's knot) enabled the lonely 'scribbling spinster' to express her fantasies and frustrations.

She also seemed to enjoy the excitement that the clandestine nature of this writing provided – it was a thrilling secret too shocking for the staid citizens of Concord, Massachusetts to know about: 'I think my natural ambition is for the lurid style,' she once confessed. 'I indulge in gorgeous fancies and wish that I dared inscribe them upon my pages and set them before the public . . . How should I dare to interfere with the proper grayness of old Concord? The dear old town has never known a startling hue since the redcoats were vehicle for her distinctive gifts. She was able to evoke a reassuring domestic warmth and intimacy, and to reveal her natural eye for detail and incident.

IMPRESSIONS OF WAR

Little Women was not Louisa Alcott's first book in this style. Five years earlier she had written *Hospital Sketches,* describing scenes she had witnessed while working as a nurse during the Civil War. The sketches were based on her own letters to her family, and were initially published as newspaper articles. They had the same vivid, episodic quality as *Little Women.* The book 'never made much money, but it showed me my style.'

There was an element of happy accident in the way *Little Women* came to be created. Louisa offered to write a volume of fairy tales, but her publisher pressed her for a girl's book; and since her father had long decried the absence of plain, domestic stories for children, the dutiful Louisa set herself to write, drawing on the material she knew best. A note in her journal conveys her initial uncertainty: 'I plod away, though I don't enjoy this sort of thing. Never liked girls or knew many, except my sisters; but our queer plays and experiences may prove interesting, though I doubt it.'

Louisa's publisher was inclined to agree with her that *Little Women* was rather unexciting; but they were both proved wrong. The book sold a million copies in Louisa's lifetime, and remains a perennial favourite despite radical changes in family life and society at large. The public demanded more, and *Good Wives, Little Men* and *Jo's Boys* followed.

Apart from their inherent qualities, *Little Women* and its sequels broke new ground. Most previous writing for juveniles reflected an authoritarian family structure in which stern Papa laid down the path of duty, and the supreme childish virtue was obedience. The March family operates on quite different lines: relationships are close, and based on mutual affection; the girls are all individuals, with distinctive traits and ambitions; and if there is still a fixed moral code ruling their lives, it is not a drill but an ideal to be taken to heart.

The March family is an idealized version of the Alcotts; in *Little Women,* tomboy Jo is a likeness of Louisa herself. And even in the later books, where there is more invention, Jo's school is conducted on the progressive, libertarian lines advocated by her father, while Jo's literary career parallels Louisa's.

'ANY PEN, ANY PLACE'

Louisa May Alcott produced many more stories and poems for children, though none rivalled the four March family books. Ideas always came easily to her, and she wrote with amazing facility. 'My head is my study, & there I keep the various plans of stories for years sometimes, letting them grow as they will till I am ready to put them on paper. Then it is quick work, as chapters go down word for word and need no alteration . . . While a story is underway I live in it, see the people, more plainly than real ones round me, hear them talk, and am much interested, surprised or provoked at their actions, for I seem to have no power to rule them, and can simply record their experiences and performances.'

In her later years Louisa Alcott still felt the compulsion to write, despite fits of impatience when she described her work as 'moral pap'. Although financially secure and in bad health, she poured out books, stories and poems, as well as magazine articles and advice columns in which she encouraged girls to be career-minded and advocated votes for women.

When writer's cramp paralyzed her right thumb, she learned to write with her left hand. And when she became seriously ill and her physician forbad her to get on with *Jo's Boys*, her supposed boredom with the March family evaporated. She noted in her journal: 'Planned *Jo's Boys* to the end and longed to get up and write it. Told Dr W. that he had better let me get the idea out then I could rest.' When she was allowed to work for half an hour a day, then two hours, she rejoiced and 'forgot my body and lived in my head'. Less than a year before she died, she set down her requirements for writing: 'Any paper, any pen, any place that is quiet suits me.'

Domestic details
Louisa's father called Orchard House (below), their home from 1858, 'a pretty retreat, and ours; a family mansion to take pride in'. Louisa's books excelled in depicting everyday family life (right).

Louisa's father, Bronson Alcott, was a philosopher who lived by a strict set of ideals which brought him inner peace and the respect of a few like-minded men, but virtually no money. Conscious of her family responsibilities, Louisa was busy with her pen even as a teenager, writing and publishing short stories and poems. But apart from *Flower Fables* (1855), written when she was just 16,

she did not publish a book until the appearance of *Hospital Sketches* (1863), based on her nursing experiences during the American Civil War. By then she had discovered that she could help to support the Alcott household by writing lurid thrillers such as *Pauline's Passion and Punishment* (1863) and *Plots and Coun-*

terplots (1865), although she never publicly admitted the authorship of these stories.

An adult novel, *Moods* (1864), was followed by the enormously successful *Little Women* (1868), which set the tone for most of her subsequent work – *Little Women, Part II/Good Wives* (1869), *Little Men* (1871) and *Jo's Boys* (1886); each presented a similarly reassuring world.

FLOWER FABLES
→ 1855 ←

Tiny winged fairies wearing cowslip hats (left and below) inhabit the magical fairytale world of *Flower Fables*. A collection of fairytales and poems, *Flower Fables* was Louisa M. Alcott's first book. It was published when she was 22, but was based on stories she had written at Concord six years earlier for Ellen Emerson, the daughter of the Alcott's protector and friend Ralph Waldo Emerson.

The fairy characters are the tiny creatures of tradition, living in close contact with bees and glow-worms, bathing in dewdrops and dining on flower-dust cakes and milkweed cream. But their stories are intensely Victorian in sentiment and morality, emphasizing the value of self-sacrifice and self-reformation. In two typical examples, the patient devotion of the fairy Violet is rewarded at last when she succeeds in melting the heart of the Frost King, and the gay, thoughtless Thistledown is redeemed through his love for Lily-Bell.

Echoing the values of Louisa's awesomely stoical and self-righteous father, Bronson Alcott, the fables are essentially about virtue rewarded, but also contain vivid images of Louisa's sense of her own sin and feelings of guilt. The book was greeted with encouraging comments from local journals such as the Boston *Transcript,* which described as 'very sweet' these 'little legends of faerie land'.

Frederick Goodall: Fairy Struck. Cecil Higgins Art Gallery, Bedford/Bridgeman

J. G. Naish: The Midsummer Fairies. Christopher Wood Gallery/Bridgeman

McMullen Collection

GOOD WIVES
◆ 1869 ◆

(left) **Sisterly love continues to be a theme** in *Good Wives*, the novel which forms the sequel to *Little Women*. Louisa called this book *Little Women, Part II*, the title always used in the United States, although in Britain it is known as *Good Wives*. Three years have passed and much has changed in the lives and loves of the March family and their neighbours. Jo March, now 19, is still a tomboy, her father is back from the Civil War, and Meg marries the quiet, steady John Brooke. Laurie declares his love for Jo, who has written a novel, but she does not return his feelings. Eventually Laurie meets Amy in Europe and finds consolation with her. Beth becomes ill again, but this time she fails to recover and the family is plunged into mourning. Then Jo, determined to contribute to the Marches' finances, takes a job at a New York boarding house run by a family friend. There, to the astonishment of most readers, past and present, she meets and marries a man who is far from being the romantic hero we might expect.

LITTLE MEN
◆ 1871 ◆

The antics of Nat, Dan, Ned, Tom, Emil and the other boys (right and below) who live at a school set up by Jo and her German husband, form the basis of this sequel to *Good Wives*. The Bhaers have taken over Plumfields, Aunt March's old home, and run their school on kindly, enlightened principles. Among their charges are Meg's twins, Demi and Daisy, and Nan, a tomboy who is continually getting into scrapes. However, the greatest challenges are two poor orphan boys – Nat, the street fiddler, who is well-intentioned, although weak and given to lying, and the tough, uncouth Dan. The worst crisis occurs when a dollar belonging to Tom is stolen; the evidence seems to point to Nat but eventually the real culprit is discovered.

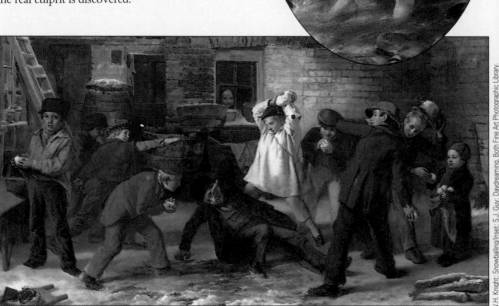

W. H. Knight: Snowballing/Inset: S.J. Guy: Daydreaming. Both Fine Art Photographic Library.

JO'S BOYS
◆ 1886 ◆

The ever-steadfast Laurie (below) has grown up in this, the last of Louisa May Alcott's March family books. The 'Little Men' are now in their twenties. In ten years, the Bhaers' little school, Plumfields, has been transformed into a fine college. Marmee has died, but Mr March, Laurie, Amy and the widowed Meg have all been drawn to Plumfields, reuniting the family. And Jo has got into her "last scrape": she has become a famous author, plagued by journalists and intrusive admirers. Despite his good heart, Dan remains restless and hot-tempered. Wandering in the West (below), he kills a man in self-defence and serves a term in prison which marks him deeply; he ends his life as the lonely defender of a mistreated Indian tribe. By contrast, Nan makes a career as one of the new breed of independent women physicians, while Nat becomes a successful musician and marries Meg's daughter, Daisy.

Compiègne/Bulloz

Frank Tenney Johnson: The Overland Trail. The Thomas Gilcrease Institute of American History and Art, Tulsa, Oklahoma

Charles Hermans: Circe. Christie's, London/Bridgeman Art Library

PLOTS AND COUNTERPLOTS
◆ 1865 ◆

The man-eating Virginie Varens (above) is the alluring temptress in *V.V., or Plots and Counterplots,* probably the most sensational of all the thrillers written by Louisa May Alcott under the pen-name A.M. Barnard. Thanks to a complicated plot involving disguises, strange family resemblances, murder and suicide, the story was successful as both a magazine serial and a ten-cent novelette. The main character is the dancer Virginie Varens, a beautiful but heartless creature who takes pleasure in tormenting the men who love her. To satisfy her desire for money and position, Virginie marries a nobleman, but the plan fails because her wealthy husband is almost immediately murdered by her insanely jealous cousin, Victor. She then turns her attentions to her husband's Scottish cousin, and succeeds in taking him from his fiancée, who responds by killing herself.

But Virginie's lurid past cannot remain hidden forever, a fact that is all the more tragic for her because she has at last fallen deeply in love – with the man whom she intended to make her victim. At the end, confronted with a choice between captivity and death, she makes a decision that is true to her own nature rather than the accepted moral precepts of the day.

North and South

The long and bitter prelude to the American Civil War focused the deep division between 'free' and slave states. The Alcotts were passionate abolitionists and played their own part in the conflict.

Louisa May Alcott was born into one of the youngest and fastest growing nations on earth. Within just 50 years of the United States winning its independence from British rule, the original 13 states of the American Union had almost doubled in number and the Republic was fast expanding westward from the Atlantic coast to the Mississippi River and beyond.

By the middle of the century the United States was confidently asserting its 'Manifest Destiny' to extend its power from coast to coast. Forty years after the first explorers, Lewis and Clark, had reached the American West Coast in 1804, large numbers of Americans were following in their footsteps, tackling the country's three greatest natural barriers – the Appalachians, the Mississippi, and the Rockies – as they created more and more territories.

But such rapid expansion in so short a time was not achieved without major problems. Two sources of conflict had been building up since the 1780s when the American Union was founded. One was the Southern states' decision to retain negro slavery (a legacy of British rule). The other was the potential conflict between individual states and the Federal Government in Washington.

Despite the fact that the American Republic had been founded on the ideal that 'all men are created equal', the Southern states of the newly formed Union demanded their right to maintain slavery – on which their thriving economy was based. The pre-Industrial South, with its huge plantations of high-yield crops of tobacco and cotton depended on its vast, cheap captive labour force. And the Northern free states (that is, where slavery was not permitted) were in no position to insist that the Southern states freed their slaves as a

Peter Newark's Western Americana

From plantation to port
(right) A Charleston wharf, piled up with cotton bales, which were literally worth their weight in gold to the land-owning few.

King Cotton
(below) The flourishing cotton plantations of the Southern states were worked by a cheap labour force of negro slaves.

BPCC/Aldus Archive

Peter Newark's Western Americana

'The Disunited States'
(left) This British cartoon of 1856 pinpointed the burning issue of slavery as the source of North-South conflict. Peace had so far been maintained by keeping a balance of free- and slave-states, but was becoming ever more fragile, with outbreaks of violence being provoked by both sides. Britain, however, was scarcely in a position to sneer. Although slavery had been abolished there over 20 years previously, in America it was the direct legacy of British colonial rule.

prerequisite of joining the Union. The South simply would not have joined, which would have drastically reduced the size and power of the new Republic. So the American Republic became a deadly compromise, living uncomfortably with slavery.

A census in 1790 showed that the United States had a population of 4,000,000 – 500,000 of whom were negro slaves. Many people in both North and South saw slavery as a regrettable phenomenon which would eventually die out of its own accord, but they were mistaken. When the invention of the cotton gin (which separated the cotton from the seed) in 1793 caused such a boom that the cotton industry became America's most lucrative export, the wealthy Southerners were even more determined to keep their slave labour force.

The runaway pace of westward expansion fuelled the conflict between North and South. The North inevitably wanted the new states to be slave-free, while the Southerners, ever eager to increase their cotton growing empire, wanted slavery to be extended. So these settler 'territories' of the expanding frontier – destined, when their populations were large and organized enough, to satisfy Congress and join the Union as fully fledged states – increasingly became first ideological, then bloody battlegrounds between pro- and anti-slavery factions.

THE MISSOURI COMPROMISE

The first real hint of conflict occurred in 1820, when there was a dispute in Missouri as to whether the territory should join the Union as a free or slave state. Missouri was the 10th new state to join the Union since George Washington's inauguration as America's first president in 1789. Of the previous nine, four had been free states: Vermont, Ohio, Indiana and Illinois. The other five – Kentucky, Tennessee, Louisiana, Mississippi and Alabama – had doubled the size of the slave-owning South in less than 30 years.

Since Missouri had been settled by pro-slavery Southerners, it was clear which way they would vote. For the first time, the North felt directly threatened, because this new slave state jutted directly into its westward-expanding path. And the Northerners were determined not to be outflanked and outnumbered by the Southern states. If Missouri joined the Union as a slave state, it would make a total of 12 slave states to only 11 free states.

Bloodshed was averted by the Missouri Compromise of 1820-21, in which the precarious free-state/slave-state balance was artificially preserved by creating the new free state of Maine on the Canadian border. This enabled Missouri to be admitted to the Union as a slave state, with the important proviso that no more slave states could be created north of Missouri's southern border.

It was the North's first successful attempt to curb the expansion of slavery, where before it had merely trusted that right would eventually win the day. The Southerners became increasingly determined to prevent a repetition of the Missouri Compromise, and to extract the utmost benefit from the Federal Constitu-

Double standards
While condemning the South for perpetuating the barbaric institution of negro slavery, the industrial North relied on its own form of cheap labour (above). European and Irish immigrants flocked to the land of promise, only to find they had no choice but to work in semi-slavery in the factories of the North (top). Lincoln commented on this hypocrisy, 'If free Negroes be made things, how long, think you, before they will begin to make things out of poor white men?'

tion, which actually tolerated slavery. The likely pattern of immigration – biased as it was towards the North – would have meant that more free states than slave states were settled. This would have made the South a minority in the Senate (where each state was represented by two senators) and made it impossible for them to block hostile legislation.

THE PROPAGANDA WAR

As well as the struggle for legislation, a propaganda war developed between North and South. Some of the North's most strident propaganda emanated from Louisa's hometown of Boston, where William Lloyd Garrison had founded *The Liberator* in 1831. In 1832, the New England Anti-Slavery Society was established; the following year saw the birth of the American Anti-Slavery Society. In contrast, the South's counter-propaganda was muted and ineffectual.

Southerners even failed to press home the propaganda opportunities that followed the abortive uprising led by the negro slave Nat Turner in 1831. The insurrection was crushed in Virginia within 48 hours, and from start to finish Turner never led more than 60 men. But the South was so shaken by the uprising that it never fully publicized and exploited the fact that Turner's defeat was ensured by the decision of local slaves to fight against him in support of their masters.

The South not only fell behind in the propaganda war, but was incensed by the illegal encouragement and aid abolitionists gave to runaway slaves. By the 1840s the North had created the 'Underground Railway', the secret route by which slaves were spirited northward to Canada and freedom. The Alcotts, like many of their friends, were passionate abolitionists, taking in their first runaway slave in February 1847 when Louisa was

Peter Newark's Western Americana

Saviour of the Union

(left) Abraham Lincoln, President 1861-65, believed passionately in personal freedom, calling slavery a 'monstrous injustice'. But he was even more dedicated to the cause of saving the Union.

14. Southerners responded to such acts by taking the law into their own hands. They pursued hundreds of escapees, proclaiming their legal right to recapture their valuable 'property'.

The country's internal conflict was briefly pushed aside when the 1846–48 Mexican War hit the national headlines. But the trouble reappeared with a vengeance after the American acquisition of California and New Mexico, and the California gold strike of 1848. The

Slave rebellion

Nat Turner (1800-31), shown here at the time of his capture, led an unsuccessful slave insurrection in Virginia in 1831. A noted preacher, he claimed that the inspiration to revolt came in a voice from heaven. In 1831 Turner and seven companions murdered the inmates of his master's house, then gathered a band of about 60 followers. Before the rebellion was put down Turner and his followers had killed more than 50 men, women and children. Turner and 19 of his associates were hanged.

Peter Newark's Western Americana

Thomas Hovenden: The Last Moments of John Brown. The Metropolitan Museum of Art, Gift of Mr & Mrs Carl Stoeckel, 1897

$150 REWARD

RANAWAY from the subscriber, on the night of the 2d instant, a negro man, who calls himself *Henry May*, about 22 years old, 5 feet 6 or 8 inches high, ordinary color, rather chunky built, bushy head, and has it divided mostly on one side, and keeps it very nicely combed; has been raised in the house, and is a first rate dining-room servant, and was in a tavern in Louisville for 18 months. I expect he is now in Louisville trying to make his escape to a free state, (in all probability to Cincinnati, Ohio.) Perhaps he may try to get employment on a steamboat. He is a good cook, and is handy in any capacity as a house servant. Had on when he left, a dark cassinett coatee, and dark striped cassinett pantaloons, new--he had other clothing. I will give $50 reward if taken in Louisvill; 100 dollars if taken one hundred miles from Louisville in this State, and 150 dollars if taken out of this State, and delivered to me, or secured in any jail so that I can get him again. WILLIAM BURKE.

Bardstown, Ky., September 3d, 1838.

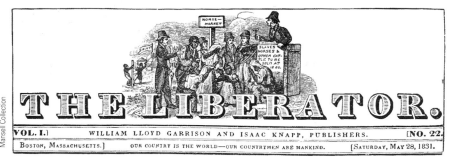

THE LIBERATOR.

VOL. I.] WILLIAM LLOYD GARRISON AND ISAAC KNAPP, PUBLISHERS. [NO. 22.
BOSTON, MASSACHUSETTS.] OUR COUNTRY IS THE WORLD—OUR COUNTRYMEN ARE MANKIND. [SATURDAY, MAY 28, 1831.

The fight for freedom

(left and above) Although it had a fairly small circulation, the Boston weekly newspaper The Liberator was a powerful weapon in the abolitionist cause. Its founder, William Lloyd Garrison (1805-79), a fanatical opponent of slavery, secured the services of distinguished authors to write for him – John Greenleaf Whittier, for example. Many slaves, however, tried to secure their own freedom by fleeing to the North.

Abolitionist martyr

(left) John Brown (1800-1859), one of the most celebrated figures in the anti-slavery movement, had intended to become a minister of religion, but instead worked at a variety of agricultural jobs. His mission in life, however, was to oppose slavery by any means. In 1856 a group of his followers killed five pro-slavers and in 1859 he tried to start a slave insurrection at Harper's Ferry in Virginia, but was forced to surrender to the marines. In this romanticized painting, Brown is shown being embraced by a negro baby on his way to execution. He was regarded as a hero in the North, and 'John Brown's Body' became a famous marching song for Union troops in the Civil War.

westward rush of prospectors and settlers once more brought to the fore the question of how such new states would align themselves.

The uneasy peace was becoming increasingly fragile. The Missouri Compromise had worked for 30 years, but by the mid 1850s, atrocities were being committed by both sides in the territory that became known as 'Bleeding Kansas'. Meanwhile, the Southern states took their argument to Washington, demanding the legal protection of slavery when the Fugitive Slave Act of 1851 proved wholly ineffective.

But central government itself was weakening, with the divisions appearing within the old political parties – the Democrats and Whigs. And the emergent Republican Party, the 'party of moral ideas', was upsetting the balance further by pledging to oppose the extension of slavery in the West.

The conflict was dramatically encapsulated in the figure of the militant abolitionist John Brown. To Southerners he was a butchering ruffian, the leader of the Kansas murder squads. To Northerners, and abolitionist families like the Alcotts, he was a crusading hero in the Lord's cause. It was in Louisa's town of Boston that Brown raised the money for his raid on Harper's Ferry in Virginia, in 1859. He hoped this would provoke a war of slave liberation, but his defeat and hanging did little to mollify the infuriated South, which regarded the raid as one more example of Yankee treachery.

After his death, John Brown passed into Northern legend as a martyr for their cause, and inspired Louisa Alcott to write:

> *No monument of quarried stone,*
> *No eloquence of speech,*
> *Can grave the lessons on the land,*
> *His martyrdom will teach.*

Her memorial poem was published in *The Liberator* in January 1860, the fateful election year which ended with the election of Abraham Lincoln as the first Republican president.

'THE WRITING ON THE WALL'

Lincoln had declared in 1858 that 'this Government cannot endure permanently half slave and half free', and that before long the country would be 'all one thing, or all the other'. Though no abolitionist, he believed that the civil rights of all citizens, regardless of race, were at stake, and said that the 'new free states' should remain so because they were 'places for poor people to go and better their condition'. But his overriding determination was to preserve the Union, and he took pains to reassure the Southerners that he would not tamper with their 'peculiar institution' where it already existed.

51

Sources and Inspiration

Nevertheless, the South saw that with the election of a Republican president, they would be unable in future to direct their own affairs, since the balance of power would be forever weighted in favour of the North. They decided that, as the Union would no longer serve their interests, they no longer wished to be part of it. Within a month of Lincoln's election, South Carolina had seceded (withdrawn) from the Union. By the time the president was inaugurated, Georgia and the five states on the Gulf of Mexico had joined South Carolina to form the Confederate States of America.

In response to the split, Lincoln determined to assert his federal authority over the Confederate States – not by violence, but with the symbolic gesture of sending provisions to the government fort in Charleston Harbour, South Carolina. The Confederates viewed the provisioning of Fort Sumter as a definite provocation, and they could not, moreover, allow a federal fort to dominate their best harbour. The Confederate General, Beauregard, therefore responded by bombarding Fort Sumter, and after 34 hours it was surrendered to him by Major Robert Anderson.

No-one was killed, but the attack polarized North and South. The issue was now simple. The North united behind Lincoln in a patriotic defence against the 'war of aggression' that the South had instigated against the 'Government established by our fathers'. The Southern Confederacy was joined by Virginia, North Carolina, Tennessee and Arkansas. The American Civil War began.

Philippoteaux: Battle of Gettysburg (detail)/Weidenfeld Archive. Top: Peter Newark's Western Americana

Division and death
The American Civil War was an appallingly bloody conflict; the North lost more than 350,000 men, the South more than 250,000.

52

KATHERINE MANSFIELD

◆ *1888-1923* ◆

An enigmatic but alluring figure, Katherine Mansfield
rejected the bourgeois respectability of her colonial
background for an independent if uncertain life in Europe.
Her youthful relish of adventure left her scarred, physically
and emotionally, but her dedication to her art survived
hardship and crippling illness. In her brief life, she remoulded
the short story according to her fine sensibility, to earn
herself a place with the most innovative of modern writers.

CAPRICIOUS CHARM

Katherine Mansfield veered from 'sunshine and gaiety' to petulant wilfulness. She saw 'power, wealth and freedom' as the means to happiness, and risked all in their pursuit.

Katherine Mansfield left her native New Zealand at the age of 20 never to return. This name was the one she adopted later and by which she became known. By dropping her father's name, she compounded her bid to escape her family and assert her independence. She found the adventure and fame she sought, but was to pay dearly for it.

Kathleen Mansfield Beauchamp was born in Wellington, New Zealand, on 14 October 1888. Colonial life at that time was marked by nostalgia for the mother country 12,000 miles away, and by the snobbish division between old established families and those who had only recently acquired wealth. Her father, Harold Beauchamp, was one such *nouveaux riches*. He made a fortune in insurance and business, ending up as a distinguished colonial banker. (He was knighted in 1923, days before Katherine died.)

As a child, Katherine became accustomed to a life of luxury and ease, but this comfort was not matched by emotional warmth. Her feelings of being rejected by her family continued all her life. Her mother was cold and distant, and tended to enhance Katherine's sense of being the 'odd one out', the most difficult and least attractive of four daughters. On her return from a business trip abroad, Mrs Beauchamp singled out her third daughter for comment, 'Well, Kathleen, I see that you are as fat as ever'. Having at last borne a male child, Mrs Beauchamp considered the family complete. The one redeeming character in Katherine's young life was her maternal grandmother. Granny Dyer was loved by all the children, and lived with them almost until her death in 1907.

In her isolation, Katherine turned inwards and began writing at a very early age. At Miss Swainson's snobbish school in Wellington, she produced her own school magazine – 'imaginative to the point of untruth' was the headmistress's unsympathetic verdict. Katherine was, in fact, a lifelong, pathological, flamboyant liar, as neglected children often are.

Katherine was contemptuous of her parents'

A wayward child
The third daughter of Annie and Harold Beauchamp (left and right), Katherine (above) was the 'ugly duckling' of the family – difficult and a lifelong disappointment to her unimaginative, bourgeois parents.

Wellington Harbour
Growing up with a beautiful, sweeping harbour (left) virtually on her doorstep, Katherine developed a love for the sights, sounds and smells of the sea.

First home
Katherine's birthplace (above) was discreetly respectable. As her father's fortunes prospered, the family moved to ever more lavish surroundings.

materialistic values. But for all she despised her father for his 'undeniable trade atmosphere', his money enabled her to leave New Zealand for boarding school in Harley Street, London, with her elder sisters, Vera and Charlotte. On the first day at Queen's College, Katherine met Ida Baker whom she later renamed Lesley Moore ('LM') and who was to remain utterly devoted to her throughout her life. The nickname was an example of Katherine's passion for alternative identities. 'Would you not like to try out all sorts of lives – one is so very small?' she once asked.

London schooldays
From 1903 to 1906 Katherine attended Queen's College (right), studying, playing the cello, and above all tasting freedom.

Key Dates

1888 born in New Zealand

1903 attends Queen's College, London: meets Ida Baker

1908 involved with Garnet Trowell

1909 Bavarian exile and miscarriage

1911 meets John Middleton Murry

1913 friendship with the Lawrences

1918 marries Murry

1920 *Bliss and Other Stories*

1923 dies in Fontainebleau

FIRST LOVE

On her return to New Zealand in 1906, Katherine fell in love with the artist Edith Bendall, with whom she said she felt 'more powerfully all those so-termed sexual impulses . . . than . . . with any man'. There were to be other important women in her life, but she soon shunned the idea of lesbianism, longing for marriage and children.

Meanwhile, Katherine pined for the culture and sophistication of London, and in 1908 she left New Zealand and sailed back to England. Three weeks after arriving, she fell in love with Garnet Trowell, a musician from her home town, whose family she had known well in New Zealand. They became engaged, but Katherine quarrelled with his parents – they were nervous of her grand,

extravagant ways, and she was scornful of their poverty (although she had only a small allowance herself). Garnet was obliged to give her up, and she rushed into marriage with George Bowden, a polite bachelor in his thirties who taught singing.

Bowden did not know, of course, that Katherine was pregnant with Garnet's baby when the wedding took place in March 1909. Having engineered this marriage of convenience, Katherine refused to consummate it. She decamped to her own lodgings on her wedding night and a few days later was on a northbound train. She joined Garnet on tour in Glasgow and Liverpool, where he was playing with the Moody-Manners Opera Company, and even performed there herself.

she was a suffragette and writer, and both helped introduce their young 'find' to the literary world, with its stimulating social life. Katherine moved nearer *The New Age* office, to Clovelly Mansions in London's Gray's Inn Road.

By 1911, the new author had symbolically dropped the Beauchamp part of her name and, as Katherine Mansfield, was beginning to acquire a reputation as a fine writer. In December of that year, a momentous meeting took place. Katherine was invited to a dinner where another guest was an Oxford undergraduate, the co-editor of the bilingual quarterly magazine *Rhythm*. Katherine was immediately attracted to John Middleton Murry, while he, already an admirer of her writing, was fascinated by her. It was particularly

Hearing of her daughter's misdemeanours, Mrs Beauchamp immediately set sail and reached London in time to whisk Katherine off to Germany, where she hoped the 'scandal' would remain a secret. Mission accomplished, she returned to England, leaving her daughter alone in Germany. Soon afterwards Katherine miscarried.

DEEP WOUNDS

Mrs Beauchamp's behaviour in abandoning her daughter, and, later that year, cutting her out of her will, marked Katherine for life. Confused and lonely, Katherine now wrote to Ida Baker asking her to send her a child to care for. Ida despatched a sickly boy called Charlie Walter, who stayed with Katherine for his summer holidays and was instructed to call her 'Sally'.

During this period Katherine met Floryan Sobieniowski, a 28-year-old aspiring writer-translator from Poland, who was on holiday in Bavaria. He introduced her to the stories of the Russian Anton Chekhov, who was then little known in western Europe. It is almost certain that Katherine caught gonorrhoea from Sobieniowski, because of which she subsequently became infertile, and suffered from arthritis, pleurisy, a weak heart and various other ailments. It also made her vulnerable to the tuberculosis which killed her.

Katherine broke off the affair abruptly, without any explanation. Sobieniowski (who might well have thought himself cured when he met her) was aggrieved, and was later to prove a dangerous man to have offended. The following year she underwent 'a terrible operation' for peritonitis, caused by an infected Fallopian tube. The surgery had the disastrous effect of spreading the infection throughout her body, and from this time on she was a chronic invalid.

Luckily, George Bowden could be persuaded to provide Katherine with a home on her return from Germany. He also provided her with her first literary outlet. Struck by the originality of her Bavarian stories, he introduced her to A. N. Orage, editor of *The New Age,* a magazine of politics and letters. Orage's guidance was of great benefit to the young writer. He and his lover Beatrice Hastings were free-thinking bohemians;

Maori country
Returning briefly to New Zealand, Katherine (standing left, above) went on a month's trek with a few 'ultra-colonial but kind-hearted' companions.

Devoted friend
Ida Constance Baker (right), nicknamed by Katherine 'LM', stood by her friend through poverty, illness and despair, happy just to serve and adore.

Chelsea lodgings
(below) From her two-roomed flat Katherine tried a singing career – inspired by her neighbour Mme Alexandra – then acting, then designing clothes, then writing.

JOHN MIDDLETON MURRY

Katherine Mansfield met John Middleton Murry in December 1911, and from then until her death in 1923 they had a tortured, tempestuous love affair.

Murry, from a humble South London background, made his way to a brilliant career at Oxford, editing an ambitious bilingual magazine, *Rhythm*. He was friendly with and deeply influenced by D. H. Lawrence, and later as editor of the *Athenaeum* published writers such as Virginia Woolf and T. S. Eliot. Although they spent much time apart, Murry was at Katherine's bedside when she died and later championed her work.

her self-possession and independence which he liked, giving him the impression that she was 'not, somehow, primarily a woman'.

Murry was to have a profound effect on Katherine's life and work. Having overcome poverty to become an outstanding scholar, he was well versed in classical and modern languages. He was also an aspiring writer, but his real gift was for editing; *Rhythm* was an ambitious venture, combining fine artwork with the newest writing in English and French.

Katherine began to contribute to the magazine, and Murry sought her editorial advice eagerly – something which brought down on her the combined anger of Orage and Hastings. They regarded this, quite irrationally, as treacherous nepotism, and began to attack Katherine in *The New Age*.

Shortly after becoming editor of the *Westminster Gazette*, Murry moved in as Katherine's lodger at Clovelly Mansions – a rival to poor Ida. Not for the first (or last) time, the devoted friend prepared for his arrival and gave generously from her own meagre purse to ensure Katherine had all she wanted.

After a short, platonic acquaintance Katherine asked Murry to 'make me your mistress' – and after some initial resistance, he did. In spite of the physical attraction they felt for each other, their sexual life was apparently inadequate. Katherine expressed a good deal of dissatisfaction on this account: 'You and I don't live like grown-up people', she once told him. This child-like aspect of their relationship was also reflected in their frequent daydreams about a perfect life together. But their relationship was in fundamental ways to remain unresolved, interrupted by Katherine's search for an elusive cure.

Impulsive and impractical, they now took a three-year lease on a cottage near Chichester, hired a man-servant and had headed notepaper printed – none of which they could afford. They stayed there little more than a month.

Meanwhile, *Rhythm* was struggling to survive, but winning some valuable contributors – despite certain errors of judgement. One issue contained a poor review of *The Trespasser* by D. H. Lawrence. Unperturbed, Lawrence submitted some sketches and stories, and thereby began a long association with the Murrys. He had just published *Sons and Lovers,* and was living with Frieda Weekley, who had left her husband and three children for him. When the two couples met in 1913, there was an immediate rapport between them. Frieda's husband was refusing to let her see the children, and Katherine provided a sympathetic ear.

There was also an immediate bond between Katherine and Lawrence which would undoubtedly have endured but for complications with their partners. Katherine said of her first meeting with him, 'All I remember is sunshine and gaiety.' Although Lawrence's working-class background differed radically from Katherine's,

Early love
Katherine's first grand passion was the shy young musician Garnet Trowell (above). She loved him, became pregnant by him, but married another.

Bavarian exile
Learning of Katherine's 'shocking' behaviour, Mrs Beauchamp sailed half-way round the world to try to allay further outrage. She whisked her daughter off to Bavaria (below), and there abandoned her to her fate.

he shared her bold irreverence, her delight in the natural world and her passion, 'without which one writes in the air'. They had considerable influence on each other, Lawrence using her as a model for several characters, Katherine planning to write a novel on the lines of *Sons and Lovers*.

The Lawrences were devastated by the declaration of war in August 1914. By contrast, Katherine and John were strangely untouched. 'We were neither for war nor against it. To be for or against a thing it must belong to one's world, and this was not in ours', wrote Murry. War was not literature, so they declined to think about it. Otherwise, Katherine could certainly not have undertaken her foolhardy expedition to visit novelist and poet Francis Carco who was fighting on the French front. She fancied she was in love with him, and the brief affair was symptomatic of her restlessness and dissatisfaction with Murry's cool English temperament. One event in the War, though, was to disturb her profoundly: her brother Leslie, to whom she had only recently become close, died in action in 1915.

It was Lawrence who understood her problematic nature and felt that Katherine and Murry would be better off apart – '[she] needs to be quiet, to learn to live alone and without external stimulant.' But despite their frequent separations, they were unable to part finally, and it is conceivable that Katherine's failing health contributed to her dependence on him.

On her own account, she was beginning to lead a hectic social life. By now acquainted with the Bloomsbury set, she was meeting a host of new, influential figures: the painter Dorothy Brett, the philosopher Bertrand Russell (who pursued her amorously), and the inimitable hostess Lady Ottoline Morrell, whose luxurious lifestyle

Mediterranean sojourn
Stricken with tuberculosis, Katherine (above right) abandoned England in search of healthier climates. She, Ida and Murry travelled to the South of France (above), hoping that sunshine, rest and clean air would work miracles. Murry soon had to return to England; Ida, ever faithful, stayed on to look after her friend.

Katherine envied. Virginia and Leonard Woolf also befriended her. They had recently set up the Hogarth Press and Leonard was anxious to further Katherine's promising career. Few have described her so perceptively: 'By nature, I think she was gay, cynical, amoral, ribald, witty. When we first knew her, she was extraordinarily amusing. I don't think anyone has ever made me laugh more . . . in some abstruse way Murry corrupted and perverted and destroyed Katherine both as a person and a writer . . . At the bottom of her mind she knew this, I think, and it enraged her . . .'

Although she acknowledged a rivalry with Katherine, Virginia Woolf felt a unique sense of

---

Fact or Fiction

GRANNY DYER

The serene, loving Mrs Fairfield, who keeps her daughter's household together in the short story *Prelude* is much like Katherine Mansfield's precious Granny Dyer. It was she who ran the Beauchamps' house and looked after the children, and Katherine's love for her is apparent throughout the story: "There was something comforting in the sight of her that Linda felt she could never do without. She needed the sweet smell of her flesh, and the soft feel of her cheeks and her arms and her shoulders still softer."

kinship with her. Katherine wrote to her, 'You are the only woman with whom I long to talk work.' And on Katherine's death Virginia felt 'there was no point in writing. Katherine won't read it.'

Once she was diagnosed as suffering from tuberculosis, Katherine searched desperately for a cure. 'There is a great black bird flying over me, and I am so frightened he'll settle – so terrified.' She travelled to France where Ida joined her. The bombardment of Paris trapped them there, and she wrote copiously to Murry – 50,000 words in three months – anticipating a joyous reunion and marriage. On her return he was so horrified by the deterioration in her appearance and so scared of her disease that instead of embracing her, he turned aside and covered his mouth with his handkerchief.

ILL-FATED MARRIAGE

They were married, however, in May 1918. By now Katherine was so ill that she was often convinced he was 'trying to get rid of her'. Time and again she made reference to her need for warmth and tenderness, reproaching Murry with mentions of attentive husbands, loving fathers. But he continued to disappoint her, failing to pay for reviews she wrote and even to remember her birthday. He grew more and more wrapped up in the hectic cultural life of Bloomsbury and made no secret of an affair with a certain Princess Bibesco while Katherine was convalescing in France. 'He ought not to have married', she wrote sadly. 'There never was a creature less fitted by nature for life with a woman.'

His was not the only treachery she had to contend with. In September 1920 she travelled to Switzerland with a £40 advance on some stories – the first substantial sum she had earned. Her old flame Sobieniowski chose this moment to black-mail her for the money, in return for some letters which referred to a Chekhov story she had plagia-rized early on. Katherine assented unhesitatingly, not wanting Murry to know about it.

A HARMONIOUS COMMUNITY

In October 1922, Katherine sought the help of the charismatic Greek-Russian George Gurdjieff. He had founded the Institute for the Harmonious Development of Man in Fontainebleau, and claimed to reintegrate the diseased minds and bodies of his patients by simple communal life and work. Katherine happily did her share of peeling vegetables, wrapped in her fur coat against the bitter cold. She sent for Murry, and when he arrived, sat with him spinning fantasies about the simple, rural life they would lead together. On the evening of 9 January, as she went upstairs, she began to cough. Suddenly a great gush of blood spurted from her mouth. 'I believe I'm going to die', she gasped. Murry rushed for help but it was too late.

Katherine was 34. In an unsent letter to Murry she ended with the words: 'No truer lovers ever walked the earth than we were – in spite of it all.'

Mary Evans Picture Library

George Gurdjieff
A charismatic personality, Gurdjieff (left) founded an institute at Fontainebleau, near Paris, devoted to harmonizing the physical, emotional and intellectual sides of human nature. His disciples grew vegetables, ran a farm and lived as an extended family. It was to this community that Katherine, after some months in the Swiss Alps (below), turned when fever and pain reasserted themselves. And it was here that she found some form of peace – a remission from fear and isolation if not, ultimately, from her fatal disease.

Sidney Herbert: The Wetterhorn from Grindelwald/Fine Art Photographic Library

BLISS AND OTHER STORIES

Three well-known stories illustrate Katherine Mansfield's most disarming qualities – her perceptiveness, compassion and subtlety – all shaped by a light, seemingly spontaneous style.

Fritz Thaulow: Rustic Farmhouse/Fine Art Photographic Library

Katherine Mansfield's stories are intensely personal; she wrote of little that did not happen directly to her. Drawing more and more deeply on her own experiences, she returned in spirit to the New Zealand of her childhood, where she found the material to shape her greatest stories. *Prelude* is one such story based on her early family life. She was equally interested in the complex, fraught and often treacherous relations between men and women, and this is reflected in one of her most famous stories, *Bliss*.

One of Mansfield's strengths is her uncanny ability to enter into the minds of her characters and convey a sense of mood or pathos through the skilful blending of interior monologue and descriptive prose. Her characters may be in materially different circumstances from her own – as is the woman in *Pictures* – but their isolation

A new home
(above) Exciting vistas open up for the Burnell children when they move to a new house, complete with a thrilling garden to explore, a verandah and a grapevine. Next morning, when the front door finally slams behind Stanley, the grandmother and her daughters set the place to rights – or idle around, according to their respective roles (right). Peace reigns, but discontent ripples the surface.

Henri Lebasque: Tea on the Terrace at Saint Maxime (detail). Christie's, London/Bridgeman Art Library

and silent struggle for survival were all too familiar to her.

PRELUDE

Katherine Mansfield's longest and best known story is set in New Zealand, among the Burnell family. Subtle and evocative, it creates a lost world of childhood in which all kinds of tiny events achieve an almost magical significance in the mind of a child.

The story is also about adults; all the characters are carefully drawn to create a strong sense of the different worlds they inhabit while yet living together under the same roof.

The story opens with a move. Little Lottie and Kezia are left to wait with neighbours for the storeman to take them to their new home that evening. Their sleepy journey under the stars sets the tone of the story. Lyrical and impressionistic, the language suggests a convergence of temperaments and personalities, shifting, colliding and settling, all in their different parts of the strange, new house and garden.

The grandmother, practical and capable, is at the centre of the children's lives. She puts them to bed, gets their breakfast

Intrepid Kezia
(right) The youngest Burnell explores the tangled garden and orchard, her imagination thrilling with wonder at the novelty.

Daydreams
(left) Lovely, lissom Beryl dreams of "a young man, dark and slender, with mocking eyes", lurking outside in the dark.

"Isabel wheeled a . . . pramload of prim dolls and Lottie [walked] beside her holding the doll's parasol . . . 'Where are you going to, Kezia?' asked Isabel, who longed . . . that Kezia might be roped in under her government. 'Oh, just away,' said Kezia."

Things domestic
(right) The kitchen becomes the grandmother's natural domain, and Linda comments, "It says 'mother' all over; everything is in pairs."

James Shannon: The Flower Girl. Tate Gallery, London

A brimming cup
Mistress of an "absolutely satisfactory house and garden" (below) and mother of an adorable baby, Bertha (left) is intoxicated with her good fortune. But how can she express her bliss "without being 'drunk and disorderly'?"

The feeling persists, burning more intensely than ever when she looks into the garden at a "tall, slender pear tree in fullest, richest bloom . . ."

The guests arrive and Bertha experiences a deep unspoken intimacy with Pearl Fulton, her beautiful new woman friend. Her feelings of elation are overpowering. Bertha suddenly desires her husband for the first time in their married life, and is impatient to be on her own with him. But there is a shock in store for her before bedtime: a surprise that mocks

T. M. Rooke: North End House, Rottingdean (detail)/Fine Art Photographic Library

and, on the first morning, turns them out into the garden to play until called. Kezia – the youngest – explores the garden on her own. Linda, her mother, drifts languidly about the house, wanting only to be left alone. Beryl, the young unmarried aunt, is unhappy at moving so far from town. She sits and plays her guitar, dreaming of love. Stanley Burnell, bustling and self-important, is proud of being able to provide such style for his family.

The title of the story implies there is more to come, and certainly Katherine Mansfield wrote more stories about the family. But there is also a sense within the story of something about to happen, which creates a curious tension. Linda Burnell, lost in a timeless past, lies late in bed, "waiting for someone to come who just did not come, watching for some-

> *"Oh, why did she feel so tender towards the whole world tonight? Everything was good – was right. All that happened seemed to fill again her brimming cup of bliss."*

thing to happen that just did not happen".

Beryl and Stanley live in imagined futures, albeit very different ones. Stanley contemplates greater prosperity and a son to complete his family. Only the children occupy the eternal present with their discovery of mystery and adventure in every waking minute. All of this is captured in Katherine Mansfield's carefully crafted prose, her means of expressing the richness of her childhood.

BLISS

Katherine Mansfield wrote extensively about men and women caught in unhappy relationships. *Bliss* is a beautifully ironic tale of marital disharmony masked by superficial perfection. It is told entirely from the viewpoint of Bertha, the young wife. She believes herself to be ideally happy, bound up in her affairs of running the house, battling with Nanny to be allowed to play with her baby, and making arrangements for a dinner party one evening. For no particular reason she is overcome that day "by a feeling of bliss – absolute bliss! – as though you'd suddenly swallowed a bright piece of that late afternoon sun and it burned in your bosom".

In the Background

THE ALOE

In *Prelude*, the weird aloe plant symbolizes fierce independence. Its medicinal powers, and the fact that it flowers rarely ("Once every hundred years", says Linda) lend it a fascination that instinctively Kezia senses.

ALOE ARBORESCENS.

Mary Evans Picture Library

> *"'Give me back that letter. Give it back to me at once, you bad, wicked woman,' cried Miss Moss, who could not get out of bed because her nightdress was slit down the back. 'Give me back my private letter.' The landlady began slowly backing out of the room, holding the letter to her buttoned bodice."*

all she has been feeling that day, and the very basis for her sense of joy and wonder.

Bliss captures the excitement and naiveté of a young woman on the brink of discovery. Poised on the edge of a new experience, casting her mind back over all the things she knows and loves, Bertha is beside herself with anticipation. Much of the story's perfection lies in Mansfield's use of language and symbolism to evoke Bertha's awakening sexuality. The story has a breathless intensity, punctuated with Bertha's sudden shifts of attention and gasps of excitement. The slender flowering pear tree under the silver moon is the outward manifestation of all that Bertha is feeling:

"Although it was so still it seemed, like the flame of a candle, to stretch up, to point, to quiver in the bright air, to grow taller and taller as they gazed – almost to touch the rim of the round, silver moon."

The pear tree's shimmering beauty remains unchanged, however, while Bertha herself suffers a shattering revelation.

PICTURES

Pictures is a wonderfully compassionate portrayal of a woman alone in the world without means or protection. Ageing, tired Ada Moss is out of work and owes her landlady rent. A one-time contralto singer in West End musicals, she is forced to seek any kind of acting work. She has until eight o'clock that evening to pay her rent, and so starts out early doing the rounds of the agents.

Dismissed without thought by everyone in the business, she still does not lose her optimism. The absurd application form of one film agency reduces her to tears, but a good cry "cheered her wonderfully". There is only one place left for her to go in search of money, and she faces her last resort ever hopeful of being 'discovered'.

Mansfield explored this theme of bereft womanhood in many of her stories. Sometimes the woman is young and vulnerable, as in *The Little Governess* and *The Tiredness of Rosabel*. At other times she is

Rude awakening
Harrassed by her landlady for overdue rent, Ada Moss (right) is torn between fury and humiliation. "Oh, if I could only pay that woman, I'd give her a piece of my mind that she wouldn't forget."

Bright lights
Armed with "one and thrippence" for a cup of tea, Ada tries her luck in London's West End (below).

W. R. Sickert: *Yvonne*. Christie's, London/Bridgeman Art Library

C. H. W. Nevinson: *The Strand by Night*. Bradford City Art Gallery & Museums/Bridgeman

old and still defenceless in a hostile world.

Drawing very much on her own difficult experiences in London during her early twenties, Mansfield conveys in *Pictures* the hungry need for money and love with painful accuracy. Ada Moss's desperation is never made explicit. The sense of her miserable life is built up in tiny details. She cannot get out of bed in front of her landlady because her nightdress is torn. With only one and three in

her bag she is happy at the thought of a cup of tea in an ABC café. Buoyant with a belief in her own talent and ability to find work, her true predicament as a faded, unemployable, second-rate singer gains all the more in poignancy.

Ada Moss's perpetual tussle with her unsympathetic landlady has a grim, sordid reality. She is painfully aware of being treated with contempt because she has no money:

" 'Oh, if I could only pay that woman, I'd give her a piece of my mind that she wouldn't forget. I'd tell her off proper.' She went over to the chest of drawers for a safety-pin, and seeing herself in the glass she gave a vague smile and shook her head. 'Well, old girl,' she murmured, 'you're up against it this time, and no mistake.' "

Many of Mansfield's characters possess this quality of pathos. Victims of a harsh world, they have a softness concealed under a determined bravado that makes them touchingly vulnerable. As Ada Moss says to herself:

"Why shouldn't I go to the Café de Madrid? I'm a respectable woman – I'm a contralto singer. And I'm only trembling because I've had nothing to eat to-day."

CHARACTERS IN FOCUS

With just a few deft phrases, Katherine Mansfield creates vivid, beguiling characters, capturing something of ourselves with her astute perceptions. Through interior monologue and unusual narrative techniques, Mansfield conveys the innermost person, taking us into the very hearts and minds of her characters, to explore their secret lives.

WHO'S WHO
PRELUDE

Kezia Sensitive, bright and fanciful, she is the youngest in the family.

Linda Burnell As wife and mother, she seems deeply unsuited to both roles, taking refuge in her alleged frailty.

Stanley Burnell "The soul of truth and decency", he is the pompous, well-meaning provider, adoring his wife and children.

Grandmother Fairfield "Always so fresh, so delicious", she is the emotional centre of the household.

BLISS

Bertha Young Looking in the mirror she sees "a woman, radiant, with smiling, trembling lips . . . and an air of listening, waiting for something divine to happen."

Pearl Fulton One of Bertha's "beautiful women who had something strange about them", her cool detachment intensifies Bertha's excitement.

Harry Young Energetic and with a "zest for life", he is Bertha's much-loved husband.

PICTURES

Ada Moss Once in possession of a fine contralto voice, she is now ageing, lonely and down to her last shilling.

Mrs Pine A hard-boiled landlady, she insists that Ada must pay her rent or leave.

PRELUDE

Always dressed in linen, the grandmother (right) holds the family together with quiet and unwavering strength. She bathes "in cold water winter and summer" and is as constant and dependable as the morning sun. Kezia loves her unreservedly, but 'her Granma' is without favourites, looking after everyone – her unhappy daughter Linda as well as her granchildren – with equal vigilance.

T. Barrett: Summer Afternoon Tea (detail). Phillips Auctioneers/Bridgeman Art Library

Mary Cassatt: Mother and Child (detail). Private Collection/Bridgeman Art Library

Similar in temperament, Linda and her daughter Kezia (above) both live in their imaginations, escaping to private places where no-one else can reach them. But Kezia's is a joyous world, rich in secrets and discovery, while her mother's is much darker, a place of chronic discontent. The two are not close, Linda being too whimsical and self-centred to be interested in her "three great lumps of children". But Kezia can amuse herself alone for hours.

As a businessman rooted in the material world, Stanley Burnell (right) is the complete antithesis of his wife. He views his family as an extension of himself, needing only a son to make it complete. Linda likens him to a Newfoundland dog, "For she really was fond of him; she loved and admired and respected him tremendously . . . He was the soul of truth and decency, and for all his practical experience he was awfully simple, easily pleased and easily hurt."

Illustrated London News Picture Library

Barnes: Portrait of a Young Lady. Towneley Hall Art Gallery/Bridgeman Art Library

Ambrose McEvoy: Blue and Gold/Fine Art Photographic Library

BLISS

Excited, high-spirited and easily moved, Bertha Young (centre) is pent-up emotion and sexuality. "Although [she] was thirty she still had moments . . . when she wanted to run instead of walk, to take dancing steps on and off the pavement . . . or to stand still and laugh." Intoxicated with life as she is, she cannot quite communicate her feelings to her adored husband.

In some ways Bertha's 'second self', Pearl Fulton (left) is mysterious and deeply sensual. "She seldom did look at people directly. Her heavy eyelids lay upon her eyes and the strange half-smile came and went upon her lips as though she lived by listening rather than seeing."

PICTURES

"I'm just the same full figure as I used to be", comments Ada Moss (right), yearning for a "Sensible Substantial Breakfast". But she remains cheerful in spite of its absence, and struggles to maintain her courage and good humour in the face of seemingly insurmountable odds – hunger, poverty, and blows dealt by thoughtless casting agents.

A. H. Maurer: Model with Japanese Fan (detail). Private Collection/Bridgeman Art Library

SUBTLE PERCEPTIONS

Katherine Mansfield devoted her career almost exclusively to the short story, her gently penetrating style making it an exquisite vehicle for her observations of the human condition.

'Oh to be a *writer*, a real writer given up to it and to it alone!' Katherine Mansfield recorded this cry of despair towards the end of her short life, in February 1920. It reflects the fact that ill health and financial and emotional problems frequently distracted her in the course of a literary career that was to last little more than a dozen years. As a result, her output was small: 73 completed short stories, plus a handful of poems, some bread-and-butter book reviews, and her letters and journals – often hurriedly pencilled scrawls, not written with publication in mind.

Katherine Mansfield is one of the few major writers to have worked almost exclusively in the medium of the short story. In her time, as now, publishing a novel conferred far more prestige on an author than the most exquisite of stories, and Mansfield did on occasion make serious attempts on the longer form before abandoning the effort. Significantly, *Karori*, her planned New Zealand novel, eventually broke up into *Prelude, At the Bay* and other associated but separate stories. Although illness and lack of time may have encouraged her to concentrate on the short story, it was also the form that best suited her preoccupation with small, apparently ordinary but intensely illuminating moments. These had previously been treated by poets rather than prose writers, and to convey her intended subtleties of feeling and atmosphere Mansfield had to achieve a poem-like verbal concentration and precision.

A SLOW WAY FORWARD

'In *Miss Brill* I chose not only the length of every sentence, but even the sound of every sentence. I chose the rise and fall of every paragraph to fit her, and to fit her on that day at that very moment. After I'd written it I read it aloud – numbers of times – just as one would *play over a musical composition* – trying to get it nearer and nearer to the expression of Miss Brill – until it fitted her.'

Katherine Mansfield was a true innovator, breaking with the established tradition that made plot and character the overriding concerns of fiction. 'No novels, no problem stories, nothing that

is not simple, open' was her declared aim. But just because none of her English contemporaries were moving in a similar direction, her own way forward was slow and uncertain.

Her first collection of stories, *In a German Pension* (1911), was sufficiently conventional for her to dismiss it later as 'positively juvenile'. This is unfair to a series of entertaining sketches, mainly drawn from her experiences in the small Bavarian hotel where she stayed when pregnant by Garnet Trowell. Her vivid pictorial style is already present, and the satire on German habits is effective, if rather heavy-handed, with a neat, anecdotal quality that Katherine Mansfield came to feel was 'a lie'. During World

War I, when anti-German feeling was strong, a publisher suggested that a new edition of *In a German Pension* would be profitable, but she refused to consider it.

The *German Pension* stories originally appeared in the periodical *The New Age*. Her very first contribution, *The-Child-Who-Was-Tired,* concerned an overworked and exhausted servant girl who is driven to stifle a baby that will not stop

Devoted artist
Completely devoted to the profession of writing, Katherine Mansfield (above) prided herself on her capacity for work, which not even illness could blunt: 'without work I would commit suicide.'

Influential editor
(left) Alfred Richard Orage was the editor of the prestigious journal The New Age. *It published work by established authors such as G. B. Shaw and H. G. Wells, as well as by talented unknowns like Katherine Mansfield.*

Childhood memories
(right) Mansfield's stories were often inspired by her childhood in New Zealand, when reading and writing formed an escape from her affection-starved life.

crying. Only after Katherine Mansfield's death was it generally noticed that the story was virtually identical with a tale predating hers by the great Russian writer Anton Chekhov. This plagiarism (possibly unconscious) indicates the importance of Chekhov's influence.

'THE ENGLISH CHEKHOV'

Mansfield admired Chekhov greatly, helped a friend with the translation of his letters, and declared of his story *Misery* that she 'would see every single French short story up the chimney for this. It's one of the masterpieces of the world.' Towards the end of her life – and long afterwards – she was often called 'the English Chekhov'; high praise, although it undervalued her own originality.

A key episode in the development of her style was probably her long struggle to complete a single story of great personal and literary significance. *The Aloe* was begun in April 1915, rewritten in February 1916, and reworked into its final form in the summer of 1918, when it was published as a booklet by Virginia and

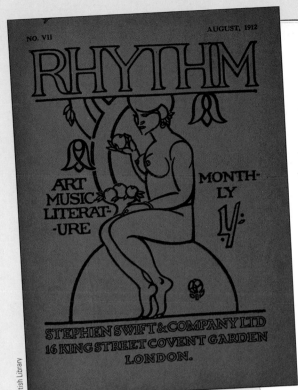

NO. VII   AUGUST, 1912

RHYTHM

ART MUSIC LITERAT-URE

MONTH-LY 1/-

STEPHEN SWIFT & COMPANY LTD
16 KING STREET COVENT GARDEN
LONDON.

British Library

THE SEA CHILD

Into the world you sent her, mother,
  Fashioned her body of coral and foam,
Combed a wave in her hair's warm smother,
  And drove her away from home.

In the dark of the night she crept to the town
  And under a doorway she laid her down,
The little blue child in the foam-fringed gown.

And never a sister and never a brother
  To hear her call, to answer her cry
Her face shone out from the hair's warm smother
  Like a moonkin up in the sky.

She sold her corals; she sold her foam;
  Her rainbow heart like a singing shell
Broke in her body: she crept back home.

Peace, go back to the world, my daughter,
  Daughter, go back to the darkling land;
There is nothing here but sad sea water,
  And a handful of sifting sand.

KATHERINE MANSFIELD.

Emil Czech: 'Children in a field of flowers/Fine Art Photographic Library

Mansfield the poet (above) The periodical Rhythm was a short-lived (1911-13) but brilliant outlet for avant-garde writing and art, and included the work of painters such as Picasso. Mansfield's own contributions included the poem above.

Russian mentor Anton Chekhov (below) was one of the outstanding dramatists of the late 19th century and one of the greatest of all short-story writers. Katherine Mansfield admired him enormously and was unquestionably influenced by him.

Novosti Press Agency

Leonard Woolf. By this time its title had been changed to *Prelude*. This is the finest of Mansfield's stories, and none of her other works cost her so much trouble. It marks her realization – probably triggered by the death of her brother on the Western Front – that she had 'a perfect passion' for the native land which she had once been so desperate to leave. Henceforward memories of New Zealand would be one of the most powerful emotional springs of her writing. 'I want to write about my own country till I simply exhaust my store . . . Oh, I want for one moment to make our undiscovered country leap into the eyes of the Old World.'

Prelude has all the qualities of Katherine Mansfield's mature art – a plunge straight into the story without preamble, a strong visual quality, seemingly fragmentary and unrelated episodes, objects that acquire symbolic significance, and a mysterious

tend to be set in lodgings or trains or cafés, often on the Continent, reflecting her own rootless existence with Murry and her travels in search of a cure for her failing health.

MEMORIES AND EMOTIONS

The principal character is usually a woman on her own, a prey to fears and strangers (like *The Little Governess*) or isolated within one or more insecure and unreliable relationships. *A Dill Pickle,* inspired by an encounter with a former lover, brilliantly conveys the kaleidoscope of memories and emotions beneath the surface of a meeting that has no 'practical' outcome. In *Je ne Parle pas Français* the characters are undoubtedly based on Murry, the writer Francis Carco and Katherine Mansfield herself. The events are fictional, devised to bring out most clearly the truth of this triangular relation-

ship as Katherine Mansfield saw it – the weakness of Dick/Murry and the curious depravity of Raoul/Carco.

A similar imaginative projection lies behind *The Man Without a Temperament,* which describes the desolate life in exile of a husband who has devoted himself to looking after his invalid wife – something that Murry could not or would not do. The story was written in a single day, as a strangely oblique response to a 'night of misery' at Ospedaletti when she felt that 'J. had no more need of our love.'

ENDURING INFLUENCE

Her relationship with Murry was the emotional centre of Katherine Mansfield's life, and he was of practical help in finding her outlets for her stories; but his literary influence on his more gifted wife seems to have been slight. After Katherine Mansfield's death, however, Murry's determined efforts and his stature as a critic ensured that she was not forgotten. During her lifetime she had published only three collections; as her literary executor Murry issued two more collections, plus editions of her journals, letters and book reviews, as well as writing books and articles of his own about her.

Murry's emotional exhibitionism laid him open to the suspicion that he was trying to cash in on his dead wife's fame, and Aldous Huxley drew a cruel portrait of him as the nauseating Burlap in *Point*

Mary Evans Picture Library

Living by the pen
(left) *'More even than talking or laughing or being happy, I want to write',* said *Katherine Mansfield, who like her rival Virginia Woolf fought resolutely to achieve respect in a man's world.*

sense of fluctuating sensations at play behind outward events. Replying to a friend who asked 'What form is it?', she replied 'As far as I know, it's more or less my own invention.'

Although she was capable of poignant insights into the lives of strangers – in *Pictures,* for example – Katherine Mansfield is essentially an autobiographical writer, drawing most effectively on her own feelings and experiences. With the exception of her New Zealand writings, her stories

On the move
(right) *Mansfield spent a great deal of her life travelling. In her journal she recorded the pleasure she took in observing fellow passengers and the places she saw – experiences that she put to good use in her stories.*

Counter Point (1928). Murry certainly wallowed in guilt feelings, and created a misleading image of Katherine Mansfield as a sweet, almost saintly figure. Recent biographers have shown her as a more flawed but also more interesting, tough-minded person. We may not quite agree with Murry that she was 'the most wonderful writer and the most beautiful spirit of her time', but her originality and enduring influence on the 20th century short story are beyond question.

Although her career was so brief, Katherine Mansfield introduced a new kind of short story into English literature – one in which traditional plots and characters are less important than revealing, poetic evocations of ordinary but significant moments. Her first collection, *In a German Pension* (1911), was relatively conventional. A number of later works also displayed Katherine Mansfield's close observation of social life; *Pictures* gives a comic and compassionate account of an ageing singer's plight, and in *Bliss* (collection 1920) family happiness proves to be based on an illusion.

The Man Without a Temperament is characteristic of Mansfield's mature style, conveying emotional realities that underlie seemingly innocuous events. Many of her finest stories in this vein hark back to her childhood in New Zealand, including her first undoubted masterpiece, *Prelude*. In *The Stranger* (The Garden-Party collection 1922), based on a shipboard death encountered by her mother, the drama is over before the beginning of the story but lingers on. In a few pages, the tragi-comic *Daughters of the Late Colonel* evokes the entire lifetime of two spinsters; while *Je Ne Parle Pas Français* (1918) is a *tour de force* in which Mansfield assumes the role of disreputable male narrator, creating a subtle, curiously poignant tale, where the 'action' is less important than deeds intended but never carried through.

THE SISTER OF THE BARONESS
←1911→

The snobbish, gross, complacent inhabitants of a small hotel in a Bavarian spa town (right) are Mansfield's targets in her first collection, *In a German Pension*, which includes this story. When the manager announces that the Baroness von Gall is sending her little daughter – who is dumb – for a 'cure', the entire establishment is set in a flutter. The child arrives, accompanied by a tall young girl who introduces herself as the baroness's sister. Although the daughter is rather unlovely, the new arrivals receive the homage of all the guests. 'The poet from Munich' is stirred to write verses to the baroness's sister, and 'the student from Bonn' courts her. But an unexpected visitor alters everything.

H. H. La Thangue: The Connoisseur (detail). Bradford City Art Gallery & Museums/Bridgeman Art Library

C. M. Pearce: Conspiracy, Café Verrey. City of Manchester Art Galleries

JE NE PARLE PAS FRANÇAIS
←1918→

Raoul Duquette, a 26-year-old Frenchman, sits in a dirty café (left) recalling an encounter that plagues him with might-have-beens. He is a writer, though often contemptuous of his own pretensions and literary mannerisms.

At a literary party he meets an Englishman, Dick Harmon, with whom he forms an ambiguous friendship, feeling himself to be a 'little perfumed fox-terrier' at Dick's disposal. Dick abruptly disappears, but later writes asking Raoul to arrange accommodation for him and a young woman.

A haggard Dick arrives with a charming girl nicknamed 'Mouse', but he is hampered by emotional ties to his elderly mother and immediately deserts Mouse. Her simple declaration – Je ne parle pas français – makes a great impression on Raoul. The Frenchman carefully insinuates himself into the position of her only reliable friend; yet it is he who ensures that the denouement anticipated by the reader does not take place.

THE DAUGHTERS OF THE LATE COLONEL
◆ 1922 ◆

The mistakes, memories and confusions of two middle-aged spinsters (below) make up this funny, painful story. 'Con' and 'Jug' are no match for the late Colonel's nurse. Even their own servant Kate despises 'the old tabbies'. They have not been able to nerve themselves to clear out the Colonel's room. Who shall have his watch? Dare they get rid of Kate? Such questions dominate as the Colonel once dominated them. Only for a moment does Con realize that glimpses of sea and moonlight have more to do with her real self than the decades of servitude to the late Colonel.

THE MAN WITHOUT A TEMPERAMENT
◆ 1920 ◆

The story encompasses a few oppressive hours in the life of Robert Salesby (above), an Englishman staying with his invalid wife Jinnie at the Pension Villa Excelsior. Pettiness and triviality reign there, and the other guests are hostile or indifferent. While Jinnie rests, Robert walks. Despite the November sunshine, his mind goes back to a happier evening, surrounded by friends, in England. He is three minutes late in returning and finds his wife coughing. Later, sitting on the balcony, recalling the doctor's verdict, he ponders the weight of his responsibility. Once more his reverie is interrupted by his wife . . .

THE STRANGER
◆ 1922 ◆

Awaiting the arrival of a liner (right), John Hammond, a prosperous, middle-aged man, feels oddly nervous. He has come to meet his wife Janey who has been in Europe visiting their eldest daughter. When the liner fails to dock and the doctor's launch goes out to it, Hammond's impatience intensifies. Successive trivialities frustrate his desire to have his wife to himself. But when they are finally alone together, Janey still withholds the spontaneous signs of affection he craves. She is preoccupied, she explains, because a passenger on the liner died in her arms – a revelation that has a devastating effect on John Hammond.

THE NEW WOMAN

Ignored, derided and abused, the first women to claim a political voice met with fierce opposition. But the 20th century brought a new breed of woman unwilling to take 'no' for an answer.

Before sailing from New Zealand to England in the summer of 1908, Katherine Mansfield had written in her diary that she was looking for 'power, wealth and freedom'. In London she would find many other women demanding the same.

England in the early years of the 20th century was full of rebels and London was the centre of their activities. The years leading up to World War I were years of tremendous political upheaval. In 1908, a Liberal Government under Prime Minister Herbert Asquith had been returned with an unprecedented majority, but it soon found itself assaulted by labour unrest, the Irish question, and a new and militant wave of women's rights advocates.

For a rebellious, middle-class woman the period was one of exhilaration, excitement and growing freedom as a new generation of independent women fought their way on to the centre stage of English political life. For eight years, from 1906 to 1914, women were barely out of the news – their exploits, demands and militancy being lampooned and attacked by the Press.

THE RIGHT TO VOTE

The demand for the vote was at the heart of the political struggle at this time. New Zealand had granted women the vote in 1893, but in Britain women were still denied their right to participate in government. This was not due to lack of effort – since 1867 constitutional suffragists had been lobbying and campaigning for the women's right to vote, using respectable and law-abiding methods. But their efforts had been to no avail: successive private members' bills had been either laughed out of Parliament or sternly rejected.

By 1908, however, when Katherine arrived in London, a new mood was sweeping the country and the women's suffrage movement had taken a dramatic and exciting turn. In 1903 a new suffrage society had been formed in Manchester, the Women's Social and Political Union (WSPU), co-founded by Mrs Emmeline Pankhurst and her daughters Christabel, a law student, and Sylvia, an artist and socialist. The WSPU had as its aim the 'immediate enfranchisement of women by political means'. From the very first it broke with tradition and adopted militant tactics. The cam-

Sir William Orpen: A Bloomsbury Family, Scottish National Gallery of Modern Art

In the background
The role of the Victorian woman was to marry, bear children and unobtrusively to keep house (above). She had to subordinate her energies, her talent and her ideas to those of her husband.

Votes for Women
Demonstrations for electoral representation (right) were met with remarkable violence. Derided by the Press, suffragettes published and distributed (below) their own material promoting their cause.

Mary Evans/Fawcett Library

paign first came to public attention in 1905 when Christabel and her companion Annie Kenney, a young cotton worker, stood up at a Liberal Party rally in Manchester and asked what was to become a famous question: 'Will the Liberal Government give votes to women?' Immediately the hall erupted; the two young women were thrown out and then arrested. They chose imprisonment instead of fines, and 'Votes for Women' was front page news.

MILITANT MEASURES

In 1906 the WSPU moved their headquarters to London, to small offices in Clement's Inn. By 1910 their offices had grown to 37 rooms, they had opened a bookshop in Charing Cross Road, and their weekly meetings attracted so many women that they regularly filled the Queen's Hall. Militancy was their keynote. Inspired by the charismatic Mrs Pankhurst and led by the autocratic Christabel, the 'Suffragettes', as they became known after an insulting article in the *Daily Mail,* embarked on a programme of propaganda and confrontation.

Their daring tactics caught the imagination of a new generation of idealistic and impatient women, many of them young middle-class educated women weary of orthodox methods for effecting change. Urged on by Christabel, the suffragettes lost no opportunity in challenging the Government and in seeking publicity. They heckled public meetings and rushed the Houses of Parliament. At their most militant they smashed windows in London's West End and in Downing Street, burned down churches and Scottish castles,

set pillar boxes alight and flooded the organ in the Albert Hall. Suffragette slogans were to be found everywhere, even burned in acid on golf courses. Obviously their efforts met with considerable hostility from police, press and Government.

PRISON TACTICS

Week after week the streets around Westminster were the scene of violent battles between women and the police, reaching a peak in 1910 on 'Bloody Friday', when for hours large numbers of women tried to push their way past mounted police to the steps of the House of Commons, asserting their right of peaceful petition. The women were brutally beaten about their faces, breasts and shoulders and otherwise knocked around, until, after public protests, police arrested 150 women and a few men, most of them bruised or injured. Women continued to be arrested in their hundreds and they deliberately sought arrest, provoking it by spitting at police officers or slapping them in

The Pankhursts
Emmeline Pankhurst (above) founded the Women's Social and Political Union (its emblem inset) – to demand 'immediate enfranchisement by political means'. To achieve their aim, however, the Union's members felt they had no option but to resort to progressively more militant tactics.

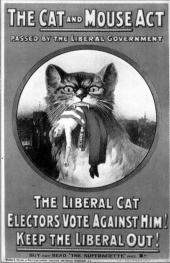

Vociferous demands
Christabel Pankhurst haranguing her critics and inciting supporters to 'rush the House of Commons' (left) was not typical of all suffragettes. Many favoured the quieter methods of peaceful campaigning, non-cooperation and boycott. But the various groups often laid aside their differences and came together in large demonstrations. It became plain that the cause had massive support.

the face. By 1914 more than 1,000 women had been imprisoned, and at one stage Holloway Prison was so full of suffragettes that the composer Ethel Smyth formed them into a choir.

From 1909 imprisoned suffragettes adopted hunger striking as a protest against the Government's refusal to give them the status of political prisoners. In turn the Government introduced forcible feeding, a humiliating and dangerous procedure. In one case, Lady Constance Lytton disguised herself as a poor seamstress in order to avoid preferential treatment in prison. She starved herself and, without medical examination, was being force-fed. This made her so ill that 'she suffered frightful nausea each time, and when on one occasion the doctor's clothing was soiled, he struck her contemptuously on the cheek. This treatment was continued until the identity of the prisoner suddenly became known. She was, of course, immediately released, but she never recovered from the experience, and is now a hopeless invalid', wrote Emmeline Pankhurst.

PEACEFUL RESISTANCE

Although the most notorious, the WSPU was by no means the only suffrage society. The National Union of Women's Suffrage Societies (NUWSS) was a far larger organisation. Led my Millicent Fawcett, the NUWSS members were constitutional suffragists and believed in peaceful tactics. The Women's Freedom League (WFL) under Charlotte Despard, which split from the WSPU, also believed in non-violent action. Their campaigns centred on tax resistance, and a boycott of the 1911 census. In order to evade the returns, women up and down the country spent the night in empty houses, with wealthy friends, in colleges and gipsy caravans, at all-night parties and specially organized concerts,

even skating on the Aldwych icerink. Many returned forms saying 'No vote no census'.

Although differing in tactics, suffragists and suffragettes frequently came together in massive demonstrations full of pageantry and colour. In one of them, 13,000 women marched through the streets of London dressed in the WSPU colours of green for life, white for purity and purple for honour – notably apolitical virtues.

The struggle for the vote provided a focus for a much wider change in women's consciousness from the 1890s to the end of World War I. The suffragettes were primarily concerned with obtaining the vote, as a tangible target and symbol of women's liberation from male power. But the overall objective varied from group to group. In the words of Mrs Emmeline Pethick-Lawrence, they were fighting: 'Not for the Vote only, but for what the Vote means – the moral, the mental, economic, the spiritual enfranchisement of Womanhood'. As their campaign continued and they were driven underground, they became increasingly separatist, adopting the slogan 'Votes for Women, Purity for Men'.

Cat and Mouse
Suffragette heroism in the cells drove the authorities to desperate, cynical measures. Because detainees refused food, and force-feeding (left) was so very damaging to health, prisoners were released when they reached a low physical ebb and, once recovered, were re-arrested. Thus the Liberals hoped to avoid the adverse publicity of deaths in custody. The notoriety which the so-called 'Cat-and-Mouse' Act gained (above), however, discredited the Liberal Government's attempts to appear humane. Public opinion started to turn inexorably in favour of votes for women.

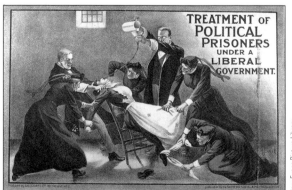

SUFFRAGETTES BATONED BY POLICE

Evening News 6.30

SUFFRAGETTE RAID ON THE PALACE: WILD SCENES

WESTMINSTER FINAL EDITION.

SUFFRAGETTES BURN ANOTHER CHURCH

Evening News 6.30

Fame and notoriety
Radical campaigners were glad of any publicity (left) and won it with acts of arson, riot, suicide, obstruction, public demonstration, vandalism . . . But as moderates – and men – rallied to the cause, press coverage became more even-handed.

Other women, such as Sylvia Pankhurst, took a socialist stand. She was a close friend of Keir Hardie, a former miner who was the first Labour candidate to be elected to Parliament, and who in 1893 was one the chief founders of the Independent Labour Party (ILP). Sylvia eventually broke away from Emmeline and Christabel, and became primarily concerned with the plight of the poor and the need for profound social change, rather than with the sole question of women's suffrage.

In fact the issue of the vote divided many feminists, particularly those who wanted 'adult suffrage', the vote granted independent of class lines, and those, like the WSPU, who were prepared to accept the enfranchisement of propertied women only. This in turn reflected a more profound division between those women who saw male power or patriarchy as the main enemy

Universal franchise
Sylvia Pankhurst broadened her aim to embrace socialism (right) and universal suffrage. Many other suffrage movements were predominantly middle-class; the vote for which they were agitating was held only by a restricted section of the male population. One of the Liberal Government's concerns was to keep the vast numbers of poor workers and unemployed (below) unenfranchized.

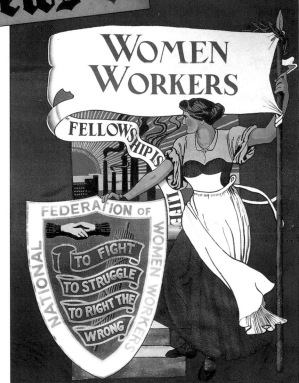

WOMEN WORKERS

FELLOWSHIP IS LIFE

NATIONAL FEDERATION OF WOMEN WORKERS

TO FIGHT TO STRUGGLE TO RIGHT THE WRONG

and those who fought for the overthrow of Capitalism – a debate that continues even today.

Other feminists were even scornful about the value of fighting for the vote. In 1914 Lily Gair Wilkinson wrote a pamphlet called *Women's Freedom*, arguing that '. . . suffragettes . . . are but a travesty of true rebel women. Rebel women struggle to be free from bondage and they struggle not against the men who share their interest, but side by side with these men'. To a great extent this was also reflected in the views of other anarchist feminists such as Lilian Wolfe and Rose and Milly Witcop. Rose Witcop in particular wrote that women were not subordinated because they did not have the vote but because they were slaves at work and in the home. They would not be freed by votes but 'by their own strength', an attitude Katherine Mansfield might well have shared.

There were also women, like Katherine herself, who were not involved in organized politics, but who were concerned – through their lives and through their art – to explore new ways of living and new, freer relationships with both men and women. These new women included Virginia Woolf, whom Katherine met in 1916. Like Katherine she too came from a wealthy and patriarchal background. In defiance of her background, she had joined the women's suffrage movement, but her ambition was to write and, by the summer of 1908, she had left London unchaperoned to stay in the provinces. This 'liberated' move was a necessary one for her, enabling her to concentrate on what would be her first novel.

PERSONAL FREEDOM

Other women who were to become important in Katherine's life included D. H. Lawrence's wife Frieda Weekley, the dashing, emancipated Beatrice Hastings and Lady Ottoline Morrell, who in 1908 was living in Bloomsbury. A patron of the arts, Ottoline Morrell played host to all the leading Bloomsbury figures of the day, including the artist Augustus John and Clive and Vanessa Bell.

Like Katherine these women were rebels, eager to achieve financial independence, to carve out their own careers and to reject the traditional stereotypes of marriage and motherhood in favour of a more unconventional and liberated lifestyle. They were privileged women – Katherine herself received an annual allowance of £100 from her father – and this certainly helped them to explore ways of living that would have been unthinkable to their Victorian antecedents. Even so these new women, unlike many others of their class, risked social ostracism by challenging convention in word or deed.

At the very heart of this search for independence was a re-examination of the relationship between the sexes, and a need to break away from conventional sexual morality. Before arriving in England, Katherine had written that 'It is the hopelessly insipid doctrine that love is the only thing in the world, taught, hammered into

Charles Shannon: The Sculptress. Musée d'Orsay, Paris/Réunion des musées nationaux

THE
NEW AGE
A WEEKLY REVIEW OF POLITICS, LITERATURE, AND ART.

NEW SERIES. Vol. IX. No. 8.   THURSDAY, JUNE 22, 1911.   [Registered at G.P.O. as a Newspaper.]   THREEPENCE.

British Library

CONTENTS.

Subscriptions to the NEW AGE are at the following rates :—

	Great Britain.		Abroad.	
	s.	d.	s.	d.
One Year ...	15	0	17	4
Six Months...	7	6	8	8
Three Months ...	3	9	4	4

SPECIAL NOTE.—All communications, whether relating to the editorial, business, advertising or publishing departments, should be addressed to THE NEW AGE, 38, Cursitor Street, London, E.C.

To the criticism of principle and detail already accumulated in these columns and elsewhere must now be added the searching analysis made by Mr. Sidney Webb and summarised in a recent issue of "The Crusade." The whole, we understand, will shortly appear in volume form. On the face of it, it may seem odd that publicists who have been advocating compulsory as distinct from optional powers in matters of industrial legislation should in the case of a National Insurance Bill be opposed to universality and to compulsion. But the reasons are plain examination. Thrift is robb ' all its virtue v' ompulsory that th ed

NOTES OF THE V

IT is so rarely that any journ honesty to acknowledge the fo against its once expressed view pleasure in reprinting the fo' "Spectator" of last week :
Some striking criticisms of th Socialist standpoint have been a' a paper which, we are glad to and independence as well as it The line of argument taken b' tendency of Mr. Lloyd Geor lation is not in the least to' It will, on the contrary, m poorer, 'l lead u' for the

New thoughts
A torrent of new ideas was loosed on Edwardian England – some of which have not been out of public debate since. The audience for such radical publications as The New Age *(above), however, was a fairly restricted artistic, well-educated circle.*

The new woman
Many intelligent women saw liberation as involving much more than the right to vote. Creative women such as Madame Bruce the sculptor (left) questioned the sexual stereotype of the 'frail sex in need of male protection and guidance'. Practically, though, it can be said that financial independence was the necessary prerequisite for the liberation of a restless, ambitious woman. An impoverished woman was still at the mercy of a male-dominated world.

women, from generation to generation, which hampers us so cruelly. We must get rid of that bogey – and then comes the opportunity of happiness and freedom!'

Much of her life was to contradict this statement, but it expressed nevertheless the same issues which were being so hotly debated in London at the time, particularly among her acquaintances. She herself contributed to *The New Age*, an aptly named radical magazine edited by A. R. Orage which featured articles on socialism, marriage reform, free love, abortion and other issues that aroused strong opinions.

OUTSPOKEN DISCUSSION

Three years later, another highly radical paper appeared, *The Freewoman*. Edited by Dora Marsden and Mary Gawthorpe, it was described by Mrs Humphrey Ward, a noted anti-feminist, as 'the dark and dangerous side of the Women's Movement'. Its contributors included Edward Carpenter, Havelock Ellis, H. G. Wells and Rebecca West, and *The Freewoman*'s outspoken discussion of marriage, divorce, free love, contraception, sexual freedom, homosexuality and lesbianism caused it to be banned from a major newsagents' chain.

In its opening issue the editors declared that *The Freewoman* marked the point at which 'Feminism in England ceases to be impulsive and unaware . . . and becomes definitely self-conscious and introspective'. It also claimed that it differed from all other journals 'devoted to the freedom of women, inasmuch as [they] find their starting point . . . in the externals of freedom. They deal with something which women may acquire. We find our chief concern in what they may become.' In their writings, their lives, and their personal experiences, Katherine Mansfield and other progressive women searched for what they might become – and in so doing paved the way for future generations of 'new women'.

VIRGINIA WOOLF

⬦1882-1941⬦

One of the most innovative writers of the 20th century,
Virginia Woolf redefined the novel, moving away from
conventional narrative to reveal her characters' thought
processes and emotional states. The intense sensitivity of her
writing reflected an acutely nervous and unstable
temperament. She inspired great love from her family and
friends, but even their devotion could not keep the terrors of
mental illness at bay.

A FRAGILE BALANCE

Poised between exuberance and despair, brilliance and the nightmare of madness, Virginia Woolf waged a lifelong battle for clarity, sanity and truthfulness.

Virginia Woolf came from a distinguished and talented family. Her father, Sir Leslie Stephen, was a noted critic and biographer and the first editor of the prestigious *Dictionary of National Biography*. He married twice; his first wife was one of Thackeray's daughters, Minny, and in 1878, three years after Minny's death, he married Julia Duckworth. She was of a similarly illustrious family and the niece of the brilliant Victorian photographer Julia Margaret Cameron. A young widow, she already had three children from her first marriage.

Adeline Virginia Stephen was born on 25 January 1882, the third child after Vanessa and Thoby. The following year, another baby, Adrian, completed the family. Virginia believed that her parents' traditions 'dashed together and flowed confused but not harmonised in her blood'. This rich mix consisted of her mother's fine sensitivity and artistic taste, and her father's equally impressive intellect. In practical terms this meant that from early childhood Virginia was immersed in an exciting and stimulating world in which she was always encouraged to read and study and express her ideas. Her imagination was early sparked into life by the family's annual

Key Dates

1882 born in London
1895 mother dies; first breakdown
1897 half-sister dies
1904 father dies
1905 first Bloomsbury meetings
1906 brother Thoby dies
1912 marries Leonard Woolf
1913 attempts suicide
1915 *The Voyage Out*
1917 starts Hogarth Press
1919 buys Monk's House in Sussex
1922 meets Vita Sackville-West
1927 *To The Lighthouse*
1941 commits suicide

Private Collection

Mother and daughter
When Virginia was 13, 'the greatest disaster that could happen' occurred – her mother Julia died. It brought her happy, secure childhood to an end, and prompted the first of many breakdowns.

holidays at St Ives in Cornwall, where Leslie had bought the beautiful Talland House. It was here that young Virginia distinguished herself as a 'demon bowler' at cricket, and indulged in the seaside pleasures of boating, fishing, and long waterfront walks.

Life was a series of adventures for the Stephen children. When Virginia was nine she embarked on a weekly paper – the *Hyde Park Gate News* – with her brother Thoby, and in play sowed the seeds of her life's work. It was not long, however, before this happy, fruitful period of her childhood came to a sudden and painful end.

When Virginia was 13 her beloved mother died. The loss was more than she could bear and caused a nervous collapse in her fragile constitution. 'The greatest disaster that could happen', as she described it, was intensified when Leslie, instead of protecting his children from the terror of Julia's death, inflicted on them his own inconsolable grief. The children's half-sister, Stella, stepped in and looked after the family, but her sudden death two years later undid the good she had done, and caused new anguish.

To make matters worse, Stella's widowed husband Jack started making passionate advances to Vanessa, while Virginia, long terrified by her half-brother George Duckworth's covertly sexual interest in her, retreated into a state of 'frozen and defensive panic'.

From being lively and outgoing, Virginia became painfully introverted and shy. It only

Inspirational summers
The Stephen children spent carefree summers at St Ives in Cornwall and years later Virginia would fondly remember the ocean's 'great plateful of blue water'.

Galerie George. London/Bridgeman Art Library

needed one more major shock to send her mad, which is precisely what happened when, in 1904, her father Leslie died from cancer. Virginia's rapidly declining nervous state was signalled, as throughout her life, by severe headaches, followed in this instance by periods of self-accusation, and the nightmarish conviction that birds were speaking to her in Greek, and that King Edward VII was hiding in the garden, muttering unspeakably foul abuse at her.

With due rest and physical care, she recovered, and, with her brothers and sisters, decided to leave behind the past and start a new, freer way of life in Bloomsbury. Yet just as they were finding their feet as young Bohemians, tragedy struck again. In 1906, after a family tour of Greece, both Vanessa and Thoby fell ill. Vanessa recovered, but Thoby, who had contracted typhoid, did not.

BIRTH OF BLOOMSBURY

Although Virginia never entirely got over her brother's death, the Bloomsbury world was starting to take shape. Her sister Vanessa married Thoby's friend, Clive Bell, and their home became a meeting place for a host of ex-Cambridge intellectuals and of talented young artists, politicians and writers. In their midst Virginia started to regain her confidence and find her voice as a writer. She began reviewing for the *Times Literary Supplement* and the *Guardian* and, at the age of 25, tackled her first novel, *The Voyage Out*.

Virginia took her writing most seriously, reworking her novel over and over again from beginning to end, but in company she was fun-loving and witty. When her brother Adrian and his friend Horace Cole devised a hoax on the

Kensington vistas
Born at 22 Hyde Park Gate, Virginia inhabited comfortable, fashionable Kensington – a far cry from bohemian Bloomsbury.

Half-sisters
When their mother died, Stella Duckworth (below centre) looked after Vanessa (left) and Virginia – and their grief-stricken father.

Royal Navy, she gladly joined in. They informed the Navy that the Emperor of Abyssinia wanted to visit the warship HMS *Dreadnought,* and then blacked their faces and donned exotic robes for the occasion. The Press was there in full force and the elaborate deception received front page coverage complete with a photograph of the '"Abyssinian Princes" who have made all England laugh'.

Almost two years later, in 1911, Virginia and her brother Adrian moved to a four-storeyed house in Brunswick Square and divided it among their friends. The economist Maynard Keynes and the painter Duncan Grant shared the ground floor; Adrian had the second floor and Virginia the third; and Leonard Woolf – the man who was to be the

mainstay of Virginia's life – took the two rooms at the top. It proved to be a propitious decision. In August 1912, Virginia and Leonard were married.

Captivated by Virginia's beauty and originality, Leonard gladly abandoned a distinguished career in the Colonial Service for her. She loved him devotedly but said with candour: 'I feel no physical attraction to you . . . and yet your caring for me as you do almost overwhelms me', a strange forewarning of the great sacrifice he would have to make. The disruptions in Virginia's childhood and the trauma suffered at the hands of her step-brother had left ineradicable scars on her. At some deep level she was frightened of men, and even under the tender, patient love of Leonard found herself incapable of any sexual response.

The Woolfs honeymooned on the Continent and returned to their separate writing ventures. Virginia completed *The Voyage Out,* and although

Greek tragedy

In 1906 the four Stephen children set off excitedly for Greece (top). They loved it, but the trip had dire consequences – Thoby (above) contracted typhoid fever and never recovered. Virginia was affected by his death for years.

the family firm of Duckworth accepted it enthusiastically, the stress of completing it induced a severe period of depression in which she lapsed from headaches to guilt and despair, seeing her nurses as fiends and degenerating into total incoherence and, finally, a coma. Recovery was slow with intermittent periods of relapse over several years

This 1913 attack was one of her worst. She attempted suicide by taking an overdose of seda-tives, and while recuperating from that, tried to starve herself to death. Leonard then, as always, played a major part in helping her through. He protected her from the outside world, and sensitively and sincerely praised her work.

PRINTING VENTURE

Clearly Virginia needed to be distracted from the demons inside her head, and Leonard, in the hope of averting further depressions, bought a small printing press on which he and Virginia began printing their own stories. The success of this venture was less the result of brilliant business decisions than of the Woolfs' store of highly talented friends and contacts, who included T. S. Eliot, D. H. Lawrence, Katherine Mansfield, Lytton Strachey, Sigmund Freud and, later, Vita Sackville-West.

In addition to the press, Virgina was kept fully occupied by her and Leonard's social life and by her varied writings which included a mammoth output of letters, reviews, essays and, from 1915 to 1941, diary entries. However, in 1921, after a relatively peaceful and productive period, she had another severe breakdown.

Virginia's diary entry of 8 August describes how she had 'two whole months rubbed out', 60

Lytton Strachey

For a heady 24 hours in 1909, Virginia Stephen and the witty, erudite Lytton Strachey (right) were engaged. The engagement was short-lived, however. Strachey panicked at the thought of being intimate with a woman, confessed his fears to Virginia and she, understanding his reluctance and knowing of his male amours, released him. They remained the best of friends, however.

Devoted sister
Three years Virginia's senior, the beautiful and talented Vanessa (above) was her sister's constant support and ally.

Sussex Downs
The calm of the Sussex countryside helped assuage the effects of London's hubbub on Virginia's delicate mental state.

LEONARD WOOLF

'**I** am selfish, jealous, cruel, lustful, a liar and probably worse still' – so the gentle, loving Leonard Woolf described himself in a letter to Virginia asking her to marry him.

Born in 1880, Leonard Woolf joined the Colonial Service after graduating from Cambridge and spent the next seven years in Ceylon, helping to govern the country. In 1911 he returned to England and to his treasured Virginia, and from then on dedicated himself to socialism and to his visionary political philosophy. He believed passionately in a new form of international government and argued his case eloquently.

His extensive literary output included two novels, but he is best remembered for his brilliant five-volume autobiography, which combines an interesting, objective account of the Bloomsbury Group, a touching portrait of life with Virginia, and a record of his fervent aspirations for a better world.

days of 'wearisome headache, jumping pulse, aching back, frets, fidgets . . . all the horrors of the dark cupboard of illness'. Aided by lengthy spells at Monk's House in Rodmell, Sussex (which they had bought in 1919), she gradually made her way out of the 'dark cupboard' and felt well enough to embark on *To the Lighthouse*.

Because of ill health, Virginia was never strong enough to write a series of major novels, and usually followed an important work with a less demanding project, what she termed a 'holiday book'. In this case it was *Orlando* and *A Room of One's Own*. *Orlando* is not just a brilliantly witty novel that transcends conventions of time and gender; it is also a veiled account of her sudden intense relationship with the writer Vita Sackville-West.

The two women had met in 1922, and although Virginia was wary of Vita's reputation as a lesbian, she eventually, after five years, developed an intensely absorbing passion for her. Although there was speculation that Virginia might leave Leonard, she stayed loyal to him, prompting Vita to the angry, incisive, semi-truthful accusation that she liked 'people better through the brain than the heart'.

By now Virginia was an immensely successful writer. *Orlando* soon sold 6000 copies. From 1929 to 1930, she made 'about £1,020 . . . a surprise to me, who was content with £200 for so many years.' *A Room of One's Own* did even better than this, selling 10,000 copies.

New money meant new possessions. The Woolfs bought a car, refurnished the house in Rodmell and began travelling abroad. There was also time off to visit her adored – and adoring – nephews and niece. She always remained in close

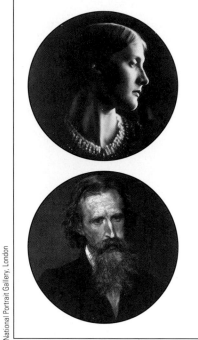

National Portrait Gallery, London

Fact or Fiction

LESLIE AND JULIA STEPHEN

Although written some 30 years after their deaths, *To the Lighthouse* was a critical tribute to Virginia Woolf's remarkable and gifted parents, Leslie and Julia Stephen. The fictional Mr and Mrs Ramsay are based on them; indeed Virginia noted in her diary before she embarked on the writing: 'This is going to be fairly short: to have father's character complete in it; and mother's.' She was so successful in her endeavour that her sister Vanessa was moved to comment: 'It is almost painful to have her [their mother] so raised from the dead. You have made one feel the extraordinary beauty of her character, which must be the most difficult thing to do.'

Pierre Bonnard: A Summer Landscape/©ADAGP, Paris & DACS, London 1989/Fine Art Photographic Library

contact with Vanessa, who, after Leonard, was the most important person in her life. All the while Virginia and Leonard were part-time publishers, printing the works of the next generation of great writers. This took up so much time that they were eventually forced to employ someone to help run the business.

Virginia's diary entry of 11 October 1929 sums up her position: 'the press is booming – & this celebrity business is quite chronic – & I am richer than I have ever been . . . If I never felt these extraordinarily pervasive strains – of unrest, or rest . . . I should float down into acquiescence. Here is something to fight; and when I wake early I say to myself, Fight, fight."

ANOTHER BREAKDOWN

The 'fight' continued with her highly ambitious revolutionary novel, *The Waves*. But she worked so intensely on it that, tired and weakened, she again had a breakdown. Initial criticism of the book did not help, but the praise which came later helped nurse her back to full health and into the attentions of her second lesbian admirer, the larger-than-life, eccentric composer Dame Ethel Smyth. Virginia wittily described how 'An old woman of seventy-one has fallen in love with me. It's like being caught by a giant crab.' But their friendship lasted just a couple of months before the intensity became too much for Virginia and she retreated into a cautious friendship with her.

Now on the verge of her 50th birthday, Virginia divided her life into two clear parts. In the country she wrote, baked bread, did gardening, and went on long rambling walks, while in London she led a hectic social life, seeing her large number of friends and fêted as the star attraction at countless dinner parties. But she was never long away from her first love, and in 1933 published

her next 'holiday' work, *Flush*, a 'biography' of Elizabeth Barrett Browning's spaniel, which she followed with her 'essay-novel' *The Years*.

Sadly, the anxiety and stress of constant rewriting induced her worst breakdown since her suicide attempt of 1913. From 10 April to 10 June 1936 her diary is blank . . . When she took up her pen again she wrote 'at last after 2 months dismal and worse, almost catastrophic illness – never been so near the precipice to my own feelings . . . I'm again on top.' But she was not. On 21 June she referred to a week 'of intense suffering – indeed mornings of torture – & . . . pain in my head – a feeling of complete despair and failure.' And on 23 June she wrote, 'A good day – a bad day – so it goes on. Few people can be so tortured by writing as I am.' Fortunately Virginia was spared further intense suffering by *The Years*' excellent reception both in Britain and in the United States.

Although the late 1930s was a time of great political unrest, Virginia's work betrayed no sign of the alarming rise of European fascism and the Spanish Civil War. She wrote at the other end of the spectrum from writers such as George Orwell and H. G. Wells, whose intent was to design a new and better world. Virginia, instead, wanted to devise a new form for the novel, relentlessly diving inside her characters, asking 'what is it like to be this person, or experience this sensation?' Nothing was real unless she could write about it. As her brother-in-law Clive Bell wrote, 'She lives in a world of fantastic daydreams, half in a world of solid reality, half in a Victorian novel.'

However, both she and Leonard were fully aware that if Hitler were victorious life would be unendurable – and together planned a suicide pact. Increasingly through 1940, as the war appeared to sway towards a Nazi victory, Virginia wondered if the time had not arrived to carry it out.

The lure of France
(above) In 1927, some of Virginia and Leonard's intimates began to make an occasional home in Cassis-sur-mer in France. The artist Duncan Grant was the first to move there, followed by Vanessa and her children, then Clive Bell and finally, briefly, Virginia and Leonard themselves. Vanessa and her family settled happily into a house called La Bergère and for three years the Woolfs toyed with the idea of joining them there, tempted by Mediterranean heat, languor and serenity. But the attractions of England and the Hogarth Press proved greater.

Strangely, she was exhilarated by the Battle of Britain, fought high over East Sussex and Kent, but appalled when the devastation hit London.

Despite these distractions she wrote on, making rapid progress with *Poyntz Hall* and a history of English literature, *Anon.* As usual, feverish spells of writing were tempered by the calm of village life, but sadly this period was suddenly destroyed in November 1940. Leonard recognized the symptoms of another impending attack.

'TROUGH OF DESPAIR'

In January 1941 her diary entries became pre-occupied with death and towards the end of the month she fell into a 'trough of despair'. Unusually, this time it was not connected with finishing a novel. There had been no warning. One moment, at breakfast, she was well; hours later she was violently excited, talking to her mother. Leonard was convinced 'that Virginia's mental condition was more serious than it had been since . . . 1913.' He knew just one wrong word could push her over the brink.

By March 27, Leonard had persuaded Virginia to see her doctor. This lady reassured her that she could survive another attack. But Virginia lost her nerve and the next day she wrote two farewell letters. One, to her sister Vanessa, spelled out that 'I have gone too far this time to come back again. I am certain now that I am going mad again . . . and I know I shan't get over it'. And to Leonard, she explained, 'Dearest, I feel certain I am going mad again. I feel we can't go through another of those terrible times . . . I can't fight any longer . . . I can't go on spoiling your life any longer. I don't think two people could have been happier than we have been.' And, having written her last words to the two people she loved most, she walked out of the house and down to the River

Vita Sackville-West
Glamorous, aristocratic and gifted, Vita Sackville-West (above) was for a time passionately attached to Virginia. With Virginia's portrait on her desk, she wrote to Clive Bell, 'I would go to the ends of the earth for your sister-in-law.'

Ouse. There, with a large stone in her pocket, she drowned herself.

A few hours later, panicked by her absence, Leonard ran to the river bank, but found only her walking stick. It was three weeks before her body was sighted in the water. After her cremation, Leonard buried her ashes at the foot of a giant elm in the garden, one of a pair which, with branches intertwining, they had affectionately named after each other. Two years later, as if to underline the tragedy, a gale ripped one of these magnificent trees out of the ground forever.

'All the happiness'
It was from the quiet of Monk's House (above) that Virginia set off one morning, walked down to the river and drowned herself. In her final note to Leonard she wrote: 'Dearest . . . I owe all the happiness of my life to you.' Leonard was to survive her by 28 years.

TO THE LIGHTHOUSE

An assortment of eccentric characters enjoy an idyllic summer, bathed in one woman's radiant influence. What changes will war, death and the passage of time make in the lives of these people?

When writing *To the Lighthouse,* Virginia Woolf said she had succeeded in 'dredging up more feelings and characters' than ever before. It is a novel in which the thoughts and feelings of the characters form the basis of the story; events are of less importance.

Virginia Woolf was fascinated by what she called 'the inner reality' beneath the surface of her characters. A remote Scottish island provides the wild and beautiful setting for an exploration of the hearts and minds of the Ramsay family and friends. The chaos of emotion behind every mundane interchange between people is made explicit, so that the characters exist in a new world of intense, introspective experience.

GUIDE TO THE PLOT
The first and longest section of the novel spans an afternoon and evening in September on the isle of Skye. It opens with Mrs Ramsay and six-year-old James, her youngest of eight children, sitting by a window. James cuts pictures out of a magazine while Mrs Ramsay knits a stocking for the Lighthouse keeper's boy. James hopes they can sail to the Lighthouse the following morning. His father, a stern philosopher concerned only with truth, smashes his son's hopes by insisting the weather will be too rough for the crossing. "Had there been an axe handy, a poker, or any weapon that would have gashed a hole in his father's breast and killed him, there and then, James would have seized it."

Mrs Ramsay is furious with her husband and his friend Charles Tansley, who merely echoes everything Mr Ramsay says. She is incensed by their indifference to the child's feelings. James is the most sensitive of all her children, and she is convinced that he will remember this moment for the rest of his

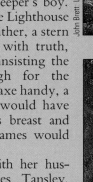

Maternal love
(left) Mrs Ramsay's bond with her children, particularly her youngest, James, is mutual. He thinks her "ten thousand times better" than his father; and she "never wanted James to grow a day older or Cam either. These two she would have liked to keep for ever just as they were . . . They were happier now than they would ever be again." So she sadly anticipates the passing of their joyful childhood.

Summer retreat
(right) Assorted guests read, think, relax and talk in the benevolent atmosphere of the Ramsays' summer home.

A child's longing
(left) James' "passion" for going to the Lighthouse is thwarted by his father's grim prediction that the weather will break.

At dinner
(right) While the conversation ranges from social pleasantries to politics, Mrs Ramsay silently muses about her life.

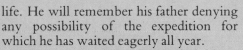

> *"Then beneath the colour there was the shape. She could see it all so clearly, so commandingly, when she looked: it was when she took her brush in hand that the whole thing changed."*

life. He will remember his father denying any possibility of the expedition for which he has waited eagerly all year.

The scene is set: mother and child are framed in the window, forming a picture of love and unity to which everyone is drawn. Mr Ramsay roams the garden, reciting poetry in fierce loud tones, surprising and alarming his guests. Unable to leave his wife alone for long, he swoops down from time to time, demanding attention. Meanwhile, their guest Lily Briscoe, who has remained defiantly single and independent in the face of Mrs Ramsay's maternal radiance, stands at her easel, wrestling with her painting. Unable to resist the picture they make, she includes the mother and son "without irreverence", as a "triangular purple shape" among the abstract forms of her work.

A STRONG FOCUS

William Bankes, another guest invited up for the summer, talks to Lily, encouraging her to join him in criticizing the Ramsays. Before she can answer, he turns to look at Mrs Ramsay and is spellbound by her beauty and power as she sits in the window with her small boy. To him her image is a reassurance "that barbarity was tamed, the reign of chaos subdued."

The children, guests and servants who fill up the house revolve like planets around Mrs Ramsay. A matriarch who is largely unaware of her power, she exerts enormous influence over the lives of those close to her. Dinner that night is a highly planned event. Bœuf en daube, the dish to be served, has been simmering for days and Mrs Ramsay is determined that everything should go smoothly. Four of the young people arrive late, which ruffles her composure, but she forgives them when she learns that there is an engagement in their midst. She believes that fulfillment on earth lies solely in love,

marriage and the creation of family life.

The beauty, charisma and sympathy of Mrs Ramsay is experienced by each character in turn. Their thoughts, interwoven with hers, gradually reveal a web of unspoken feelings. In the distance stands the Lighthouse, throwing its regular stroking beam on the house, on Mrs Ramsay as she sits exhausted in her chair, recovering from the demands of her extended family.

In the second section of the novel, the passage of ten years is described by its effect on the neglected house. It is neglected because, we are told in an aside, Mrs Ramsay has died. Wind, sea air and burrowing insects have taken their toll, as, once more, the house is prepared for its occupants.

However, nothing will ever be the same again. In the last section, the family arrive at the house with their friends. "You will find us much changed", says Mr Ramsay to Lily on their first evening. Everyone has personal discoveries to make which somehow can only happen there, with the Lighthouse beckoning in

An artist's view
Lily spends days at her easel, painting Mrs Ramsay and James as a purple shadow.

the distance. Will James reach it after all?

To the Lighthouse is in part autobiography. Virginia Woolf wrote in her diary: 'This is going to be fairly short; to have father's character done complete in it; and mother's; and St Ives; and childhood . . .' Mrs Ramsay provides a seemingly endless source of energy and life for her husband, children, dependents and friends, much as Julia Stephen did for her family.

A FREE STYLE

Although the characters are based on actual people, the novel as a whole has a lyrical quality that sets it in a tradition of its own. In dealing with the silent but powerful dynamics between people, Virginia Woolf developed a freedom of style that is still astonishing today for its fluidity and grace. The language of the novel acquires a poetic feel as it swoops and dives from person to person, taking the most mundane thought through meditation to fantasy:

"But what have I done with my life? thought Mrs Ramsay, taking her place at the head of the table . . . She had a sense of being past everything, through everything, out of everything, as she helped the soup . . ."

As she sits and ladles out the soup she is preoccupied by her strange lack of emotion for all her guests and family. Moments later, her old feelings return and she is able to smile at William Bankes sitting next to her.

People actually *do* very little in the novel; they exchange not much more than pleasant trivialities with each other. But real feelings burn just below the surface, and it is this drama of human consciousness that Woolf captures so intensely in the novel. Mrs Ramsay's ability to despise her husband one minute and worship him the next; James' hatred for his father while being desperate for his approval; Lily Briscoe's sudden swings of mood; all the contradictions and rhythms running through relationships are woven together in a completely original way.

All the main characters struggle in their different ways to establish control over their environment. During dinner, as conversation flows around him, Charles Tansley longs to retreat to his studies: "If only he could be alone in his room working, he thought, among his books." His thesis, which Mrs Ramsay describes as "the influence of somebody on something", is his antidote to human relations and the chaos and confusion they bring.

ORDER FROM CHAOS

Mr Ramsay is filled with a despairing vision of "the dark of human ignorance, how we know nothing and the sea eats away the ground we stand on", but devotes his intellectual powers to halting the tide. His rigid philosophical view of the world and his commitment to factual truth form the backbone of his identity. But none of his thoughts or academic achievements can provide him with the emotional reassurance he gets from Mrs Ramsay. She sustains him through his frequent fits of self-pity and self-doubt, giving him a vital place in the order of

"She decided that there in that very distant and entirely silent little boat Mr Ramsay was sitting with Cam and James. Now they had got the sail up; now after a little flagging and hesitation the sails filled and, shrouded in profound silence, she watched the boat take its way with deliberation past the other boats out to sea."

things once again, restoring his confidence:

"It was sympathy he wanted . . . and then to be taken within the circle of life, warmed and soothed . . . He must be assured that he too lived in the heart of life; was needed; not here only, but all over the world."

Lily's compulsion to paint comes from an impulse to make something ordered and perfect out of the fearful world about her: ". . . beneath the colour there was the shape. She could see it all so clearly, so commandingly, when she looked: it was when she took her brush in hand that the whole thing changed." When the needs and demands of people threaten to overwhelm her she retreats to her painting. The struggle to paint what she sees is immense, but it is her own struggle.

Surrounded by the clash of discordant personalities at the dinner table, Lily remembers her picture: "Yes, I shall put the tree further in the middle; then I shall avoid that awkward space . . . She took up the salt cellar and put it down again on a flower in the pattern in the table-cloth,

In the Background

STREAM OF CONSCIOUSNESS

During the first two decades of this century, a number of writers were experimenting with the novel. Besides Virginia Woolf, the Irish writer James Joyce (left) began making the thoughts of his characters, rather than plot or dialogue, the important part of the narrative. This use of 'interior monologue' or 'stream of consciousness' had a radical impact on novel-writing. For a time both Virginia Woolf and Joyce, unknown to each other, were experimenting in similar ways. Then the Woolfs were sent *Ulysses* for possible publication by the Hogarth Press. They thought it too ambitious a project for them, but Virginia paid tribute to Joyce's aims and methods.

A final trip
(left) Ten years on, Mr Ramsay, James and Cam set sail for the Lighthouse, watched by Lily Briscoe (right). "So fine was the morning . . . that the sea and sky looked all one fabric." James guides the boat towards the Lighthouse, violently longing to cut the hateful tie with his father. "But at that moment the sail swung slowly round, filled slowly out, the boat seemed to shake herself . . . and shot through the waves. The relief was extraordinary . . ."

so as to remind herself to move the tree."

Mrs Ramsay has a remarkable facility for soothing and setting things right. An archetypal mother, she is intuitive, generous, compassionate and protective. Her wisdom and ability to order her universe for herself and others comes from her belief in the heart, not the mind: "*. . . sometimes she thought she liked the boobies best. They did not bother one with their dissertations. How much they missed, after all, these very clever men!*"

Mrs Ramsay is deeply driven by her desire to create moments of order and permanence out of the chaos around her. She brings everyone together for the dinner and gives them the sense that "they were all conscious of making a party together in a hollow on an island; had their common cause against that fluidity out there".

But the effort it costs her is great: ". . . she must admit that she felt this thing that she called life terrible, hostile, and quick to pounce on you if you gave it a chance." She recovers from the endless demands by retreating into her own solitude, a "core of darkness" where there "was freedom, there was peace, there was, most welcome of all, a summoning together, a resting on a platform of stability."

AN ORDINARY MIRACLE
Mrs Ramsay's triumph is that her involvement with any activity, however mundane, lifts it into the realm of the extraordinary. Her sense of the importance of human emotion compels her to make every small occasion significant. The vitality of her children as they run about the house fills her with a sense of wonder: "Why must they grow up and lose it all?" she thinks sadly to herself. Her ability to bring people together is a skill that her friends remember. Lily has a moment of revelation as she works to finish her same picture ten years later. She recalls: "Mrs Ramsay bringing them together; Mrs Ramsay saying 'Life stands still here'; Mrs Ramsay making of the moment something permanent . . . In the midst of chaos there was shape . . ."

In the same way that Lily strives to paint the sense, the shape, and form of what she sees in front of her, so Mrs Ramsay seeks to hold on to the moments of beauty and perfection in everyday life. She has the facility that Lily needs in order to paint; the facility "to be on a level with ordinary experience, to feel simply that's a chair, that's a table, and yet at the same time, it's a miracle, it's an ecstasy".

Siblings
In adolescence the high-spirited Cam and hypersensitive James are allied against Mr Ramsay's tyranny. Cam is "fierce and loyal" to their pact, but secretly loves her father's "voice, and his words, and his haste, and his temper". James is still haunted by his mother's image. His adolescent view of reality is superimposed on his child's view, as he sees the Lighthouse at close range for the first time, and realizes that both views are true.

CHARACTERS IN FOCUS

The characters in *To the Lighthouse* form the story. What they do, what they look like, what they say to each other is of little significance. The central concern of the novel is their perceptions of the world and other people, and their unexpressed thoughts. They are portrayed through their complex inner lives, and it is impossible to make neat assessments about them, particularly Mrs Ramsay.

WHO'S WHO

Mrs Ramsay The extraordinarily beautiful mother of eight children, she is the focus and support of her family and friends.

Mr Ramsay A philosopher, who is at times "petty, selfish, vain, egotistical", but heroic in his "fiery unworldliness" and single-minded pursuit of truth.

James The youngest and "most gifted . . . most sensitive" of the Ramsay children, passionately attached to his mother and deeply resentful of his father.

Cam A "wild and fierce" seven-year-old, she is always on the wing, caught up in her own world and shying away from adults.

Lily Briscoe A struggling artist, and a friend and acute observer of the Ramsays, whom she seeks to capture in her painting.

Augustus Carmichael An ageing poet, summer guest of the Ramsays, and, interestingly, the only one immune to Mrs Ramsay's charm.

Charles Tansley A follower of Mr Ramsay and an aspiring intellectual, he is resented by the children for his mean, acidic point of view.

William Bankes A childless widower, and an old friend of the family. As cool a scientist as Lily is an artist, the two make friends but do not fulfil Mrs Ramsay's hope that they will marry.

Claude Monet: La terrasse à Sainte Adresse (detail). Metropolitan Museum of Art/Bridgeman Art Library

C. W. Furse: Portrait of a young woman. Colnaghi, London/Bridgeman Art Library

Augustus Carmichael (above) sits outside all day long, "brooding . . . till he reminded one of a cat watching birds". Large, inscrutable and dignified, he is considered by Mr Ramsay to be "a true poet".

Determined to remain true to her art, Lily Briscoe (left) resists Mrs Ramsay's insistence that she should marry – "she would urge her own exemption from the universal law; plead for it; she liked to be alone; she liked to be herself; she was not made for that . . ." Yet both women share a need to make something permanent "against that fluidity out there". Sensitive to criticism and prone to self-doubt, Lily continues her daily struggle at her easel, and finally triumphs over those who whisper, "Women can't paint, women can't write . . ."

Mrs Ramsay (left) "bore about with her . . . the torch of her beauty". Few can resist her, for "she was like a bird for speed, an arrow for directness. She was wilful; she was commanding." Yet there is a sad remoteness at the heart of her beauty and power, which makes her husband long to protect her. Her acts of charity and her matchmaking are her way of fending off the threatening chaos of "this thing . . . called life", which was "quick to pounce if you give it a chance".

At once tyrannical and child-like, Mr Ramsay (above) is "made differently from other people, born blind, deaf and dumb to the ordinary things, but to the extraordinary things, with an eye like an eagle's". For all his intellectual gifts, he needs always "to be assured of his genius, first of all, and then to be taken within the circle of life, warmed and soothed . . ." This Mrs Ramsay does, tempering his anxiety by "her laugh, her poise."

"That bundle of sensitiveness" James (left) hates the way his father's demands "disturbed the perfect simplicity and good sense of his relations with his mother". Happiness for him is his mother reading him a fairy story.

United with James against Mr Ramsay, Cam (above) is dreamy and independent, and only responds – reluctantly – to her mother. She dashes about, full of her own thoughts, "impelled by what desire, shot by whom, at what directed, who could say?"

FINDING A VOICE

For Virginia Woolf, writing was a perpetual struggle against self-doubt, criticism – and orthodox techniques. But she triumphed over the odds, her poetic style breaking new ground.

'Why admit anything to literature that is not poetry?' Virginia Woolf asked her diary in 1928, as she gathered ideas for *The Waves,* the most poem-like of all her novels. She had already broken new ground in fiction, rejecting the 'appalling narrative business of the realist: getting on from lunch to dinner: it is false, unreal, merely conventional'. Like most innovators, she was harsh in her judgement of the previous generation – in this case materialistic Edwardian 'uncles' such as H. G. Wells, John Galsworthy and Arnold Bennett

Childhood recollections
Although To the Lighthouse *is set in the Hebrides, the inspiration was St Ives (below), where Virginia spent many childhood holidays.*

who so successfully manipulated their narratives. Virginia Woolf was also averse to their generally optimistic outlook. To her, in fact, the certainties of everyday life seemed to be 'like a little strip of pavement over an abyss'.

In her view, reality consisted of a series of mental events quite unlike the neat narratives of supposed realism. 'Examine for a moment an ordinary mind on an ordinary day. The mind receives a myriad impressions – trivial, fantastic, evanescent, or engraved with the sharpness of steel. From all sides they come, an incessant shower of innumerable atoms . . . life is a luminous halo, a semi-transparent envelope surrounding us from the beginning of consciousness to the end.' It is the task of the novelist to convey 'this

Carl Holsoe: Woman Reading by Lamplight/Fine Art Photographic Library

Walter C. Hutton: The Harbour, St Ives/Fine Art Photographic Library

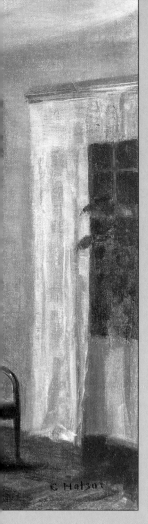

Freedom to write
(left) Virginia Woolf was greatly concerned with the prejudices and disadvantages which women writers have had to overcome. In A Room of One's Own *she maintained that women would be able to work freely only when they had financial independence and privacy.*

T. S. Eliot
The great American-born poet (right) was one of Virginia Woolf's illustrious literary friends whose work she and her husband published.

wryly admitted, quoting a fellow author, 'the worst of writing is that one depends so much upon praise'. Despite the fact that she depended heavily on the judgement of her husband Leonard, he was allowed to read her work only at a late stage in the publishing process, when the first set of proofs had been printed.

'THE CERTAINTY OF FAILURE'
Surprisingly, Virginia Woolf was subjected to few of the critical attacks so often inflicted on pioneers. Her poetic novels were received with respect, and *Orlando* (1928) and *A Room of One's Own* (1929) sold well and made her a good deal of money. In the intervals between conceiving and writing poetic novels Virginia Woolf published a number of 'holiday' and 'fact' books. *Orlando* was the happiest of her 'holiday' books, dashed off in a few months and inspired by her love for the flamboyant Vita Sackville-West, who actually makes an appearance, photographed as Orlando, in the original edition. Some other books of this sort proved as stressful to write as the poetic novels – notably the apparently light-hearted 'biography' of Elizabeth Barrett Browning's spaniel, *Flush* (1933), and a family chronicle novel aptly named *The Years,* which Virginia Woolf laboured over from 1932 to 1936, 'every morning a

varying, this unknown and uncircumscribed spirit' in all its complexity.

After publishing two relatively conventional novels, *The Voyage Out* and *Night and Day* (1919), Virginia Woolf embarked on her first serious experimental writing in a number of short stories, collected as *Monday or Tuesday* (1921). There followed *Jacob's Room,* the first novel in which she abandoned conventional narrative links. But it was in *Mrs Dalloway* and *To the Lighthouse* that she perfected her technique for recording the mind's ramblings through interior monologues which represented the 'stream of consciousness'. These captured the fragmentary, discontinuous nature of experience, and also those luminous 'moments of being' that Virginia Woolf believed were often more important to human beings than the most dramatic outward events. Stripped of conventional props, exquisitely written and carefully crafted, her novels do indeed have an affinity with poetry.

A DIFFICULT VOCATION
Virginia Woolf was utterly dedicated to writing, although for her it was a difficult and even dangerous vocation: 'Few people can be so tortured by writing as I am.' After 'that battle *Jacob's Room,* that agony – all agony but the end – *Mrs Dalloway*', most of *To the Lighthouse* came relatively easily, though only after she had suffered a temporary collapse. Virginia

Woolf's fragile health was at risk during the writing of many of her novels.

Apart from the struggle to create, she suffered agonies of self-doubt that grew stronger as the work went on. They surfaced again after publication, when she waited anxiously for the verdicts of the reviewers and of friends such as E. M. Forster and Lytton Strachey. As she

London life
Virginia Woolf described London as 'the passion of my life', and she gained much of her inspiration from observing its streets and people.

Writing and publishing
Virginia Woolf had the great advantages of ideal working conditions and freedom to publish what she chose through her own company, the Hogarth Press. At left she is shown in her London home in Tavistock Square; above is the room at Rodmell where she did most of her writing, and at right are contemporary book covers for the Hogarth Press designed by Vanessa Bell.

headache, and forcing myself into that room in my nightgown; and lying down after a page: and always with the certainty of failure.'

By contrast, Virginia Woolf's contributions to the *Times Literary Supplement* and other periodicals were despatched with the regularity of a professional journalist. Behind these essays, however, lay an immense breadth of reading, and only the fame of her novels has hindered recognition of Virginia Woolf as a great literary critic. An equally high place is likely to be taken by her diaries, which have only been published in full – to great acclaim – over the last few years. Written hurriedly, in odd moments snatched from a busy professional and social round, they provide a wonderfully fresh and spontaneous account of Virginia Woolf's life, work and friendships between 1915 and her death in 1941.

Given her temperament and experimental approach to literature, it was a

stroke of good fortune for Virginia Woolf that she was not bound by the normal author-publisher relationship. She and her husband ran their own publishing house, taking on innovative and experimental authors and poets as well as political, philosophical and esoteric pamphlets, translations of Russian classics and such illustrated works as Virginia's own *Kew Gardens*. Thanks to the existence of the Hogarth Press, she 'was the only woman in England free to write what I like'.

MILITANT FEMINISM

Other women were much less free, as she realized, and some of her most influential writing was militantly feminist. *A Room of One's Own* makes a witty onslaught on male privilege, pointing out how women have been handicapped by their inferior status and, in their writing careers, by the lack of privacy that goes with their mothering and housekeeping roles. Hence the importance to a woman writer

of 'a room of one's own and £500 a year'.

A Room of One's Own originated as a set of lectures delivered at one of the women's colleges at Cambridge. There was a gratifying irony in this, since Virginia so resented her father's failure to enter her at the university to which her brother and many male friends had automatically been sent. She nevertheless loved the city, and it is one of the main settings of her fiction, along with the Cornish landscape of her childhood and the endlessly varied London scene. For although Virginia Woolf is supremely the novelist of the inner life, she also had a strong sense of place and time. The 'feel' of England, both past and present, pervades novels such as *Orlando* and *Between the Acts*. Collectively, her essays constitute a virtual history of English life and literature. Her own writing, too, for all its innovations, has become part of the English literary tradition that Virginia Woolf herself called 'the long procession'.

After a long, largely self-taught apprenticeship, Virginia Woolf began her career as a novelist with the sensitive but relatively conventional *The Voyage Out* (1915). Her third novel, *Jacob's Room* (1922), represented a new departure, dispensing with continuous narrative and relying instead on an impressionistic build-up of images. This led Virginia Woolf to develop a 'stream of consciousness' technique in *Mrs Dalloway* (1925), where the reader is taken inside the minds of her characters. Her supreme achievement, *To the Lighthouse* (1927), was followed by a spirited historical romp, *Orlando* (1928), which was dedicated to her close friend Vita Sackville-West, a woman of similarly ambiguous sexuality to Orlando.

Virginia Woolf's experimentalism culminated in the extremely formal organization of *The Waves* (1931). *Between the Acts* promised a further development of her powers, but death intervened and the book was published posthumously in 1941, marking the end of a dazzling achievement.

THE VOYAGE OUT
◆ 1915 ◆

Rachel Vinrace, a sheltered and immature 24-year-old (right), boards her father's steamer and sets sail for South America. Among her fellow-passengers are the politician Richard Dalloway and his wife Clarissa (appearing later in *Mrs Dalloway*), who introduce Rachel to a smart, fashionable world and inadvertently initiate her emotional education. On reaching the ship's destination, Santa Marina, Rachel meets the would-be novelist Terence Hewlet. Both he and Rachel are reluctant to abandon a single life, but their developing love is undeniable . . .

JACOB'S ROOM
◆ 1922 ◆

Cambridge undergraduate Jacob Flanders beavers away in his room (below) in a scene from this unconventional, impressionistic novel. The book opens in Jacob's childhood. He is with his mother, the recently widowed Betty Flanders, on the beach, where she is writing tearfully to a friend, unaware that to a nearby painter her presence is merely an irritating, random item in a landscape. Meanwhile, little Jacob's world is filled by encounters with a crab and an animal's skull. Scenes follow of Jacob at different moments in his life: as a writer, a lover, a traveller – and, at last, as the son and friend who dies.

MRS DALLOWAY

←1925→

A party in fashionable London (right) is the focus of this experimental novel. We read the thoughts of the hostess, Clarissa Dalloway, as well as seeing her through the eyes of others. Clarissa feels an affinity with an unknown stranger – Septimus Warren Smith, a young ex-soldier driven mad by the horrors he has seen. At her party, she learns of his suicide, but though deeply shaken she remains 'the perfect hostess'.

THE WAVES

←1931→

Lyrical descriptions of the rhythm of the waves (below) punctuate the episodes in this ambitious work, often regarded as the most intensely poetic of all Virginia Woolf's books. In it, characters weave in and out of each other's lives from childhood to middle age. There is very little 'story' in the conventional sense, but the lives and personalities of the six friends around whom the novel is built are subtly evoked through their inner reflections.

J. E. Blanche: Piccadilly Circus. ©DACS 1989. City of York Art Gallery/Bridgeman Art Library

Archibald Barnes: By the river. Christie's. By courtesy of the Bourne Gallery

BETWEEN THE ACTS
→ 1941 →

At a country house, Poyntz Hall, the local villagers are mounting their annual pageant (right), a celebration of English history devised by the eccentric Miss La Trobe. As it unfolds we glimpse the tangled relationships at the Hall, notably between Bartholomew Oliver and his widowed sister, the religious, intuitive Lucy Swithin. The fraught partnership between Oliver's son Giles and his wife Isa meanwhile prompts them into mental infidelities with Mrs Manresa and Rupert Haines, a neighbouring farmer.

Despite nerve-racking moments, the pageant is a success, although Miss La Trobe is already too immersed in new plans to feel her triumph; and at the end of the day Giles and Isa retire to fight and make love.

Although the novel is set in the depths of the countryside, it reverberates with violent echoes from the war-torn world outside.

Walter Richard Sickert: A Theatrical Scene. Christie's

Far left, Detail of the sons of the Fourth Earl of Dorset. Courtesy Lord Sackville

ORLANDO
→ 1928 →

The transformation of Orlando from man to woman (far left and left) is just one facet of this amusing romp through history. As a glamorous 16-year-old boy, Orlando lives after the lusty Elizabethan fashion. In James I's time an unhappy affair with a Russian princess puts him in a more sombre frame of mind; and over the centuries Orlando's mood continues to mirror that of the period in which he lives. However, a startling change occurs during the reign of Charles II: Orlando goes into a trance and awakes as a woman. The female Orlando lives on, boldy frequenting 18th-century literary society until the Victorian age turns her into a timid, shrinking, crinolined figure. Romance then arrives in the person of Marmaduke Bonthrop Shelmerdine, who marries Orlando before leaving for distant parts. Only in the 20th century are husband and wife reunited. The original edition included photographs of Vita Sackville-West variously posed as Orlando (left).

THE BLOOMSBURY GROUP

Attracting the most brilliant personalities and advanced thinkers of the day, the Bloomsbury Group broke with Victorian convention in the search for new styles of art, literature and life.

The name of Virginia Woolf is often identified with the group of artists, writers and intellectuals who were her closest friends. This circle of intelligent and gifted people, who came to be called the Bloomsbury Group, included such famous names as Clive Bell, Leonard Woolf, Lytton Strachey and Maynard Keynes. Disparate as they were in personalities and interests, they relied much on each other for social and creative stimulus. Together they sought new ways of thinking and living, and expressed a natural and necessary reaction to Victorian convention and intolerance.

In her own writing, Virginia Woolf certainly drew on the fresh ideas that were discussed in the Bloomsbury heyday. But she, like every other member of the set, developed her own distinctive vision and style. As she became an established writer, so she depended less on the Bloomsbury Group for inspiration, yet their habit of meeting to talk and air views remained a way of life for her. In her early adulthood, however, Bloomsbury gave her the kind of intellectual freedom and interaction that she needed, just as it provided her elder sister Vanessa with the lifestyle she sought to become a fully fledged painter.

EARLY BLOOMSBURY

In 1904, on the death of their father, the Stephen children – Vanessa, Thoby, Virginia and Adrian – moved from the family house in Hyde Park Gate to 46 Gordon Square, London WC1. This move from their stuffy Victorian home to unfashionable Bloomsbury symbolized a rejection of their own social background, and, by implication, its values. It brought down on their heads 'screams' of protest from at least one old family friend, Kitty Maxse.

Thoby had recently graduated from Cambridge, and was now studying to become a barrister. He maintained contact with his university friends, however, and on 16 February 1905, he invited one of them – Saxon Sydney Turner – for an evening chat. On this occasion the only other member of the party was Gurth the sheepdog, but so began the regular Thursday evening gatherings of the Bloomsbury Group. The circle expanded as a matter of course, to include other Cambridge friends of Thoby, in particular the talented Lytton

Strachey, Clive Bell and Maynard Keynes.

All of these people were to achieve renown in different fields: Strachey as a critic and biographer, Bell as an art critic, and Maynard Keynes as a political economist of enormous influence. Apart from the fame that awaited them, these men were linked by the intellectual influences of Cambridge, and had all been inspired by the philosophy of G. E. Moore, whose work *Principia Ethica* constituted a rejection of received ideas and conventions. He maintained that: 'By far the most valuable things . . . are . . . the pleasures of human intercourse

National Portrait Gallery, London

Cambridge roots
(above) The Bloomsbury Group developed from student friendships formed at Cambridge University, where several members had belonged to the prestigious, semi-secret Apostles' club.

National Portrait Gallery, London

Leading lights
Apart from being the most influential economic thinker of his generation, Maynard Keynes (above) was renowned for his generosity and energy as a patron of the arts. His interests explicitly refuted the accusation of some critics that the Bloomsbury Group's aesthetic indulgence bypassed all social or political issues. Late in life Keynes became the first chairman of the Arts Council. Other founder members of the Group were Clive Bell and Lytton Strachey (right).

Vanessa Bell
The move to Bloomsbury was largely pioneered by Vanessa Stephen, Virginia's elder sister, who sought a liberated lifestyle in order to paint. Her homes with her husband Clive Bell, and later with Duncan Grant at Charleston, were hives of industry and talk, focal points of Bloomsbury life.

very fashion-conscious, no longer had to care about what they wore, with the result that old acquaintances were more shocked than ever. Kitty Maxse exclaimed: 'How awful they do look!', and Henry James, an erstwhile friend and admirer of Leslie Stephen, deplored the new company that Virginia and Vanessa kept. But for the young women in question, there was no looking back. Bored and oppressed as they had been by the social requirements of their former life, they took it stoically that they might be – and were – 'cut' by former acquaintances. They were more than compensated by the kind of informal 'education' that they gained from their new associations – an enriching stimulus of which Virginia particularly had felt the lack, when her brothers went off to Cambridge. But now she was their equal. 'Never have I listened so intently to each step and half-step in an argument. Never have I been at such pains to sharpen and launch my own little dart,' she declared.

The structure and development of Bloomsbury altered in 1906 on the tragic and sudden death of Thoby. Soon afterwards, his sister Vanessa married Clive Bell and settled with him at the house in Gordon Square, while Virginia moved with Adrian to nearby Fitzroy Square. Here their

and the enjoyment of beautiful objects . . . it is they . . . that form the rational ultimate end of social progress.'

All the members of the Bloomsbury Group were united by a love of literature and the arts, and, as Clive Bell later wrote, '. . . they shared a taste for discussion in pursuit of truth and a contempt for conventional ways of thinking and feeling, contempt for conventional morals if you will.' Rebellion against Victorian morality and traditional wisdom together with freedom of expression and discussion were therefore the keynotes of the Bloomsbury Group, and these attitudes and ideas were savoured and digested during their evening conversations along with coffee, whisky and buns. One of the most radical aspects of the Group was that women took a central and active part in these discussions.

INVIGORATING TALK

For the first time in their lives, Virginia and Vanessa were not required to be decorative adjuncts at a social gathering, but were expected to contribute to energetic and searching conversation as equals. The two young women who had failed miserably as debutantes now began to shine, and even to startle their male counterparts with glimpses of their originality and wit. It was a heady experience, and Vanessa later wrote, 'You could say what you liked about art, sex or religion; you could also talk freely and very likely dully about the ordinary things of daily life . . . life was exciting, terrible and amusing and one had to explore it thankful that one could do so freely.'

With this relaxation of verbal restraint went a disregard for dress. Virginia and Vanessa, never

Bloomsbury life
When the Stephens moved to Bloomsbury (right), it was an unfashionable area. Above, Virginia is shown on the roof of 38 Brunswick Square with Leonard and her brother Adrian, in a painting by Duncan Grant.

Sources and Inspiration

Influential critic

The self-portrait of Roger Fry (left) shows him as a talented painter, but he was much more important as an art critic. He ardently championed modern French painting, and organized two famous Post-Impressionist exhibitions in London, which introduced the work of artists such as Van Gogh, Gauguin and Cézanne (right) – Fry's favourite painter – to the British public. The initial reaction was mainly one of outrage ('a swindle') and contempt ('a bad joke'), but Fry's advocacy (he was a brilliant lecturer and writer) turned the tide of critical opinion.

neighbour was the painter Duncan Grant. His presence in the group lent greater emphasis to its interest in art, and this was given a dramatic new direction by another connection with an older artist, Roger Fry.

Fry was already a celebrated figure in the art world and had been Curator of Paintings at the Metropolitan Museum in New York. In 1906, he 'discovered' the work of the great French painter Cézanne and, fired with enthusiasm for his work and that of young contemporary French painters, Fry hired the Grafton Galleries in 1910 and gave London its First Post-Impressionist Exhibition. This was the Edwardian public's first taste of an entirely new depiction of reality, and, almost without exception, they hated it.

A PRINCIPLED MINORITY

Roger Fry was soon the object of violent public wrath, and became public enemy number one in the art world. The Bloomsbury Group – and, in particular, Vanessa and Clive Bell and Duncan Grant – rallied to his defence. In so doing, they ranged themselves against a staid but powerful majority, in support of artists now considered to be among the greatest of modern painters. Roger Fry became closely involved with Bloomsbury, and in turn, influenced it enormously, as he did the public's taste – whether they liked it or not. A lover of all things French, he established links between Bloomsbury and the artistic world of Paris, and familiarized them with the work of Picasso, Matisse and Bonnard.

In 1912, Fry mounted the Second Post-Impressionist Exhibition, for which Leonard Woolf, newly returned from Ceylon, acted as secretary. This show was received as badly as the first, and Leonard Woolf recorded with disgust: 'Large numbers of people came to the exhibition,

OMEGA WORKSHOPS·LTD 33 FITZROY SQ·W·

YOU ARE INVITED TO AN EXHIBITION OF DECORATIVE ART AT THE ABOVE ADDRESS; EXAMPLES OF INTERIOR DECORATIONS FOR BEDROOMS NURSERIES ETC, FURNITURE, TEXTILES, HAND-DYED DRESS MATERIALS TRAYS FANS AND OTHER OBJECTS SUITABLE FOR CHRISTMAS PRESENTS

Omega Workshops

In 1913 Roger Fry founded the Omega Workshops (right), an interior design and furnishing company that attempted to bring modern art into everyday life. The workshops were also meant to provide poor young artists with a regular source of income. Some Omega designs are now highly regarded (the screen far right, painted by Roger Fry himself, is a splendid example), but the Workshops failed commercially and were closed in 1919 amid an undignified scandal.

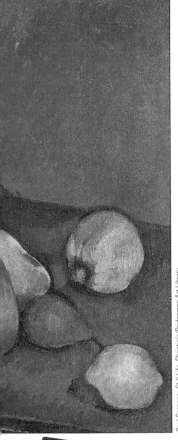

Paul Cezanne: St II Life. Christie's/Bridgeman Art Library

Duncan Grant: Self-Portrait. Scottish National Portrait Gallery.

and nine out of ten of them either roared with laughter at the pictures or were enraged by them . . . The whole business gave me a lamentable view of human nature, its rank stupidity and uncharitableness . . . Hardly any of them made the slightest attempt to look at, let alone understand, the pictures . . .' This blind contempt was the reaction to a roomful of Cézanne watercolours, 'two enormous pictures of more than life-size figures by Matisse and three or four Picassos'.

The following year, Fry founded the Omega Workshops, with a view to applying modernist design to furniture, textiles, pottery and so on, while giving penniless young artists a form of income. Vanessa Bell, Duncan Grant, the artist Wyndham Lewis and Roger Fry were supported in this enterprise by Lady Ottoline Morrell, a flamboyant and sympathetic patroness of the arts. Despite its admirable intentions, however, Omega did not survive, partly because of a smear campaign that was conducted against Roger Fry by Wyndham Lewis. Although his charges of dishonesty and double-dealing were not only answerable but actionable, Fry did not pursue the

Duncan Grant

A versatile painter and decorator, Grant was one of the first British artists to be influenced by modern French painting. This self-portrait dates from 1918.

A more constructive and benevolent attitude that was common to Bloomsbury was tolerance. In Virginia Woolf's celebrated book *A Room Of One's Own,* she argues for an alternative kind of women's liberation from the suffragette school of protest. The Emmeline Pankhurst of literature, she says, "will write in a rage when she should write calmly. She will write foolishly where she should write wisely. She will write of herself where she should write of her characters."

Here she is by no means dismissing the suffrage movement, but talking of the problems of writing in protest about anything. Virginia Woolf was typical of Bloomsbury in that she believed ideas should be born of the cross-currents of argument in which there is no conspicuous victor.

During the 1920s, Bloomsbury was very much at the centre of intellectual and literary life in London. This was largely due to the founding of the Woolfs' Hogarth Press, which published many Bloomsbury works as well as those of outside theorists and writers. Among its most influential publications of this period was Lytton Strachey's humane but critical appraisal of the Victorian age, *Eminent Victorians;* Maynard Keynes' analysis of Europe after World War I, *The Economic Consequences of the Peace;* and Roger Fry's *Vision and Design.*

Clive Bell's book *Civilisation* and Leonard Woolf's tract on individual attainment – 'A Civilised Man' – further developed the Bloomsbury quest for social identity and purpose. As in their conversation so in their writing: both men tackled the question of civilization in a

Roger Fry: Provençal Valley Screen/Anthony d'Offay Gallery

matter. Omega was finished, and Wyndham Lewis permanently estranged.

This kind of superior detachment has laid the Bloomsbury Group open to the charge of isolationism and elitism. But they were often pushed into this position by the very rigidity of the Establishment, even if they did 'enjoy' their own sense of superiority.

Sources and Inspiration

Eccentric patroness
Striking in looks and eccentric in character, Lady Ottoline Morrell (left) played host to the Bloomsbury Group, and to many other writers, artists and intellectuals, in her homes in London and Oxfordshire.

Charleston farmhouse
In 1916 several of the 'Bloomsberries' settled at Charleston (below), which became the Group's favourite country retreat. The studio (below left) was used – and decorated – by Duncan Grant and Vanessa Bell.

opted to work on the land. Lady Ottoline Morrell threw open her country estate, Garsington Manor, to such pacifists as these. For the same reason, Vanessa Bell moved with Duncan Grant to Charleston Farmhouse in Sussex. Within walking distance of the Woolfs' home, Charleston continued to be a country retreat and meeting-place for the Bloomsbury Group and many distinguished friends, long after it had served its purpose as a place of political sanctuary.

Charleston was decorated by various members of the Group, including Duncan Grant, who made it his home until his death in 1978 – he was the last of the 'Bloomsberries' to survive. By this time there had been a great revival of interest in the Bloomsbury Group, following a period when they were generally dismissed as elitist, and even accused of being a kind of intellectual mafia, protecting their own interests against outsiders. Opened to the public, Charleston has become a popular place of cultural pilgrimage.

rational way, but from totally opposed positions. Leonard Woolf was a socialist who believed that civilization had to be rooted with the masses, rather than imposed by Church or State. Clive Bell was an elitist who, though against violence, believed that civilization was the prerogative solely of a cultured class, whose existence had to be sustained at all costs by the excluded majority.

They were writing in the aftermath of a shattering world war, and their preoccupation was with understanding and so averting the forces of dissolution. Similar ideas underlie Virginia Woolf's work. She invariably sees aggressive threats to a peaceful, fruitful existence as specifically masculine. In *A Room of One's Own* she writes, "I began to envisage an age to come of pure, of self-assertive virility, such as . . . the rules of Italy have already brought into being." In *Orlando*, her ingenious and witty solution to the problem of political and sexual strife is to make the central character a man who wakes up one morning to find himself transformed into a woman.

WAR AND PACIFISM
During World War I, many of the Bloomsbury Group – including Clive Bell, Lytton Strachey and Duncan Grant – were conscientious objectors, and when conscription was introduced in 1916,

BIBLIOGRAPHY

Annan, Neol, *Leslie Stephen: The Godless Victorian*. University of Chicago Press (Chicago, 1986)

Baker, Ida, *Katherine Mansfield: The Memories of LM*. Salem House (Topsfield, 1986)

Bell, Quentin, *Virginia Woolf: A Biography*. Harcourt Brace Jovanovich (San Diego, 1974)

Bennett, J. G., *Gurdjieff: A Very Great Enigma*. Samuel Weiser (York Beach, 1984)

Bruns, Roger, *Abraham Lincoln*. Chelsea House (Edgemont, 1986)

Cheney, Ednah D., *Louisa May Alcott*. Chelsea House (Edgemont, 1981)

Crabtree, Derek and Thirlwall, A. P., eds., *Keynes and the Bloomsbury Group*. Holmes & Meier (New York, 1980)

Crone, Nora, *A Portrait of Katherine Mansfield*. State Mutual Book and Periodical (New York, 1986)

Dumond, Dwight L., *Antislavery Origins of the Civil War in the United States* (reprint of 1959 edition). Greenwood Press (Westport, 1980)

Elbert, Sarah, *A Hunger for Home: Louisa May Alcott and Little Women*. Temple University Press (Philadelphia, 1984)

Fitzgerald, Percy, *Jane Austen: A Criticism and Appreciation*. Folcroft (Folcroft, 1973)

Gara, Larry, *The Liberty Line: The Legend of the Underground Railroad*. University Press of Kentucky (Lexington, 1961)

Glendinning, Victoria, *Vita: The Life of Vita Sackville-West*. Knopf (New York, 1983)

Gordon, Lyndall, *Virginia Woolf: A Writer's Life*. W. W. Norton (New York, 1986)

Halperin, John, *The Life of Jane Austen*. Johns Hopkins University Press (Baltimore, 1984)

Hankin, C. A., *Katherine Mansfield and Her Confessional Stories*. St Martin's Press (New York, 1980)

Holroyd, Michael, *Lytton Strachey: A Biography*. Penguin Books (New York, 1987)

Kirk, Irina, *Anton Chekhov*. G. K. Hall (Boston, 1981)

Kraditor, Aileen S., *The Ideas of the Woman Suffrage Movement 1880-1920*. W. W. Norton (New York, 1981)

Laing, Donald A., *Clive Bell: An Annotated Bibliography*. Garland Publishing (New York, 1986)

Lane, Maggie, *Jane Austen's England*. St Martin's Press (New York, 1986)

Laws, Peter, *Bristol, Bath and Wells Then and Now*. David & Charles (North Pomfret, 1988)

Lea, F. A., *The Life of John Middleton Murry*. Telegraph Books (Norwood, 1986)

Lee, Hermione, *The Novels of Virginia Woolf*. Holmes & Meier (New York, 1977)

MacDonald, Ruth K., *Louisa May Alcott*. G. K. Hall (Boston, 1983)

McAleer, John, *Ralph Waldo Emerson: Days of Encounter*. Little, Brown (Boston, 1984)

Meigs, Cornelia, *The Story of Louisa May Alcott* (reprint of 1935 edition). Darby Books (Darby, 1982)

Meyerowitz, Selma, *Leonard Woolf*. G. K. Hall (Boston, 1982)

Oates, Stephen B., *The Fires of Jubilee: Nat Turner's Fierce Rebellion*. NAL Penguin (New York, 1983)

Oates, Stephen B., *To Purge This Land with Blood: A Biography of John Brown*. University of Massachusetts Press (Amherst, 1984)

Pankhurst, Emmeline, *My Own Story* (reprint of 1914 edition). Greenwood Press (Westport, 1985)

Pollock, Walter, *Jane Austen* (reprint of 1899 edition). Haskell Booksellers (Brooklyn, 1970)

Poole, Roger, *The Unknown Virginia Woolf*. Humanities Press International (Atlantic Highlands, 1982)

Rosebaum, S. P., *Victorian Bloomsbury: The Early Literary History of the Bloomsbury Group*. St Martin's Press (New York, 1987)

Shepard, Odell, *Pedlar's Progress: The Life of Bronson Alcott* (reprint of 1937 edition). Greenwood Press (Westport, 1968)

Smith, Page, *Trial by Fire: A People's History of the Civil War and Reconstruction*. McGraw-Hill (New York, 1982)

Spalding, Frances, *Vanessa Bell: A Bloomsbury Portrait*. Ticknor & Fields (New York, 1983)

Talon, Henri A., *John Bunyan: The Man and His Works*. Arden Library (Darby, 1978)

Turnbaugh, Douglas B., *Duncan Grant and the Bloomsbury Group*. Lyle Stuart (Secaucus, 1987)

Wagenknecht, Edward, *Henry David Thoreau: What Manner of Man?* University of Massachusetts Press (Amherst, 1981)

INDEX